Paul B. Kern

England 1937.

WHAT IS THE FAITH?

WHAT IS THE FAITH?

BY

NATHANIEL MICKLEM

PRINCIPAL OF MANSFIELD COLLEGE
OXFORD

LONDON
HODDER AND STOUGHTON LIMITED
1936

First Printed September 1936
Reprinted . November 1936

Made *and* Printed *in* Great Britain
By The Camelot Press Ltd
London *and* Southampton

Compellimur haereticorum et blasphemantium vitiis illicita agere, ardua scandere, ineffabilia eloqui, inconcessa praesumere. Et quum sola fide expleri, quae praecepta sunt, oportet, adorare videlicet patrem et venerari cum eo filium, sancto spiritu abundare, cogimur sermonis nostri humilitatem ad ea quae inenarrabilia sunt extendere, et in vitium vitio coarctamur alieno, ut, quae contineri religione mentium opportuisset, nunc in periculum humani eloquii proferantur.

CONTENTS

III. DOGMA

IV. NATURAL RELIGION: THE BIBLE

V. Experience : Authority

PART II: THE CONTENT OF DOGMA

VI. The Holy Trinity

VII. The Holy Nativity

X. THE ATONEMENT—*continued*

PREFACE

MY purpose in this book is to attempt an answer to the question, " How is the Christian faith to be defined? "

I have tried to avoid technicalities and to write in a popular and easy style. An author, I am told, should love his own book, but I cannot love this. It is written to serve the exigencies of the moment, not *mihi et Musis*. Those who have considered the quotation from St. Hilary which I have prefixed to this essay will understand the temper and disquietude of my own mind.

If my not infrequent lapses into the first person should cause my book to appear egotistical, I am very sorry. I should whole-heartedly agree with any critic who says that what concerns the public is the catholic faith of Christendom, not my private and peculiar ideas. But, indeed, the purpose of this book is to state, not what I believe, but what the Church believes. For myself, I desire to live and I hope to die in the Christian faith; but I know what it is to doubt, and I can very clearly distinguish between the opinions that sometimes lodge in my mind and the faith I have received. If I should cease to believe (which may God in His mercy avert!), I should be sensible of the darkening of all the lights of heaven, but I should not have to rewrite what I have written; I should still feel bound to declare, " This is the Christian faith, though I (God help me!) can no more believe it."

What, then, precisely is the Christian faith? How may

we distinguish between its unchanging essence and the various intellectual modes in which through the centuries it has been set forth? How is the form to be distinguished from the content? What is that which in any "restatement" of the faith must be restated? Is the unchanging substance of the faith necessarily to be expressed in formulæ as unchanging as itself? With these questions I shall be engaged. Thus I may presume to claim that my book is a contribution to the discussion inaugurated by the late Professor Sanday and his successor in the Lady Margaret Chair in Oxford, Professor N. P. Williams. This was published in 1916 under the title, *Form and Content in the Christian Tradition.* It will become apparent that I have a deep sympathy with the position of Dr. Williams, even though, as will be seen later, I stand in certain respects nearer to Dr. Sanday.

I have this further excuse for the occasional use of the first person: I hold a very responsible position in that branch of the Church to which I adhere. My teaching has been widely, and often quite grotesquely, misrepresented. I am under some obligation to make clear beyond cavil where I stand. I hope I have so written that for the future misrepresentation may be without excuse.

Many say, more often with pain than pleasure, that I have shifted my ground, that, whereas once I was a Liberal and a Modernist, I now am a Conservative, a reactionary, little better than a Fundamentalist or an Anglo-Catholic! I cannot persuade myself that my mental processes are of any œcumenical importance, but my intellectual pilgrimage, which, I trust, is not yet over, seems to me sufficiently typical of many as to make a brief *apologia* relevant.

Had I been uniformly consistent throughout my life

as a teacher, I should hesitate to boast of such an achievement. I hope that I have grown; I conceive myself to see some things more clearly now than I did as a young man; I could not to-day write the books and papers I could write ten or even five years ago. I do not wish to repudiate what then I wrote, but with increase of knowledge and experience my perspective has inevitably altered.

I was brought up in the fine tradition of intellectual freedom and Liberal theology. When I was a boy, the Churches of the Congregational and Presbyterian order in England and Scotland were the pioneers in unfettered theological reflection. The bonds of rigid dogmatism were being thrown off; Seeley in his *Ecce Homo* had enabled thousands to realize for the first time the true humanity of our Lord, while Harnack from Germany was demonstrating, as we supposed, that Church history between the apostolic age and the Reformation was the sad story of a Hellenizing and paganizing of the Gospel, and was offering us a version of the essence of Christianity which accorded well with the Liberalism of the period. The early Fathers of the Church, as we were disposed to think, were guilty of obscuring and institutionalizing a simple and spiritual Gospel; the theologians of the Middle Ages were hair-splitting logicians; Calvinism was no longer credible nor in any way attractive; the Roman Church was passing through the throes of its dissolution. The older and wiser amongst us, like Fairbairn and Denney and Forsyth, were, of course, delivered from this kind of crudity, but I am representing the atmosphere which we young men breathed when I was first a student of theology. I remember that for many years I thought that a Faculty of Divinity at a university was a sheer anachronism;

Church history, I supposed, was just history distorted by a bias ; dogmatics should be subsumed under philosophy of religion, and the Holy Scriptures should be treated by Christians precisely as any other literature. I had then, and I have still, a long way to go.

Shortly after the war I published *The Galilean*. I am deeply thankful for this, since under God it has been a help to very many ; but it has always been taken to be that which even then I never intended. In form it looks like a series of studies in the life of Christ, but its purpose was to answer the question, " What is religion ? " by reference to Him who is " the author and finisher of faith," the supremely religious man. The book was never intended as a contribution to the exegesis of the New Testament, still less as an essay in Christology. I could not write that book now, but I am thankful I wrote it then.

I may next refer to my chapter in the composite volume called *Mysterium Christi*. What I wrote on A Modern Approach to Christology was hailed with much satisfaction by the Liberals, and was regarded by others as a serious blot upon the book. Indeed, I note with some apprehension that, so far as I remember, that paper brought me no protest from any responsible person in the Free Churches, while later writings, in which I have appeared to be swinging towards orthodoxy, have been widely represented as a kind of treason !

I look back to that chapter, I confess, with some discomfort, not, I think, because I want to repudiate what there I intended, but because I wrote in an ignorance of which at that time I could hardly be aware. I, who might have put forward some small claim to be a scholar in matters Biblical, was criticizing theological positions which, as I now realize, I misunderstood. It is unhappily no longer possible for me to rewrite the paper.

I do not think it necessary to refer to other writings.[1] My thought has developed particularly under the stimulus of a religious situation and a theological problem which are closely related, and which, as they are strictly relevant to the subject of this book, I may here indicate.

The religious situation is this: a considerable section of Protestantism has been so eagerly advancing into new country that it has almost overlooked its duty to maintain communications with its base, or, to drop the military metaphor, it has been so concerned to accommodate the Christian faith to the modern mind that it has been relatively careless to make sure that it is the Christian faith, and not merely some mutilated fragment of it, which it has been restating. Some have, consciously or unconsciously, abandoned the Word of God contained in Holy Scripture as the standard and rule of faith, and have substituted for it human reason, or that which is called "the modern mind." They have virtually taken the view that, whatever the Christian faith may have been in the past, in future it must be that residuum which is to-day supposed to be acceptable to men of modern science. Others have adopted the principle that our duty is to abandon the traditional "religion *about* Jesus" and revert to authentic Christianity which is "the religion *of*

[1] If I could summon up interest to study the development of my thought in recent years, I should consider in this order: "The Sinlessness of Jesus," *Queen's Quarterly*, Vol. XXXVIII, pp. 219 ff.; "Dogma and Freedom," in *Essays Congregational and Catholic*; *The Historical Problem of the Gospels*, my inaugural lecture at Mansfield, privately printed; "The Theological Watershed," *Queen's Quarterly*, Vol. XLI, pp. 100 ff.; "The Holy Spirit and a New Creed," *Congregational Quarterly*, Vol. XII, pp. 545 ff.; *The Church Catholic* (Student Christian Movement Press); my chapter in *The Defence of Christianity* (Eyre & Spottiswoode), and my paper on "The Sacraments" in *Christian Worship* (Clarendon Press).

Jesus." The Jesus whose religion we are invited to adopt is almost invariably some construction of left-wing New Testament scholarship; "the Jesus of History" is assumed to be other than the Jesus of the Gospels.

Such tendencies of thought are perhaps the inevitable aftermath of a famous victory. Our intellectual liberty has been won. That was the great achievement of the last generation. To-day our problem is rather, What are the limits of that freedom, if we would continue to use the name of Christian? The intellectual chaos into which Protestantism has fallen is nowhere more effectively portrayed than in the late Fr. Grisar's pamphlet, *Die Litteratur des Lutherjubiläums, ein Bild des heutigen Protestantismus* (1918). The learned Jesuit did no more than summarize the divergent and indeed contradictory utterances of Protestants. No wonder that Protestantism sometimes seems to its friends as well as to its enemies to be disintegrating into rationalisms and subjectivisms and various relativities. I do not concur in this view; but the religious situation has forced me to the conclusion that Protestantism will repudiate the faith unless it can define it. What exactly is that Christian faith which it is our duty to restate, if we can, in the language of to-day?

The underlying theological problem presents itself with peculiar force to the Churches of the Congregational order. It is with us a principle that neither Church member nor minister shall be required to subscribe to any particular formulæ of the faith as a test of orthodoxy. At the same time we have always declared that our liberty is consistent with the requirement of a substantial orthodoxy. We have sometimes expressed a kind of perverted satisfaction that Congregationalism remained Trinitarian and orthodox when much of English

Presbyterianism was lapsing into Unitarianism in spite of the Westminster Confession. Our freedom from credal subscription, we have boasted, has not involved any disloyalty to the foundation-truths of the Christian faith; indeed, while nothing further has been required of communicants than a profession of faith in our Lord Jesus Christ, a general soundness in the fundamental doctrines of the Christian faith has been – at least till recently – required of ministers.

This attitude to credal subscription which is traditional with the Congregationalists is now very generally accepted. Even the Church of England, which steadfastly maintains the use of the ancient creeds, permits in fact considerable diversity in their interpretation, and I am convinced that Dr. N. P. Williams allows himself a latitude in respect of the Articles of his Church which he thinks reprehensible in relation to the creeds. Thus the problem which particularly besets Congregationalists concerns all Protestantism.

The Congregational principle was enunciated first in days when the final authority of Holy Scripture was unquestioned, when a massive theological system was very generally accepted, and when there was no dispute as to the fundamental truths of the Christian faith. It is no great matter to leave Christians wholly free as to the form in which they will express their faith provided that there be no dubiety as to the substance of that faith. To-day we are confronted with a very different situation. What, men ask, is really the core and substance of the faith? Must one believe in the Virgin Birth and the physical Resurrection of our Lord? Is it necessary to be a Trinitarian? Is it not permissible – is it not, perhaps, required of us – that we repudiate the theology of the apostle Paul and his successors with its insistence upon "the blood of Christ" and His eternal Godhead? Must not the authority of Scripture be wholly secondary to that of modern thought or personal religious experience? These questions are being asked, and must be asked. We are required to distinguish between the content of the Christian faith and its changing forms, between its unalterable substance and its various expressions.

In his friendly controversy with Dr. Sanday, Dr. N. P. Williams sets forth, in terms that awaken an answering echo in my own heart, his attitude to the catholic faith of Christendom on the one hand and to the claims of scientific or historical truth on the other. "*If* at any future time," he says, "an ostrakon or a papyrus leaf is unearthed at Nazareth which proves beyond the shadow of a doubt that Jesus was the son of Joseph, I shall be prepared to take the consequences. I shall frankly admit that Catholic Christianity has tumbled down with a crash, and I shall proceed to look round for some other theory of the universe. But I have a shrewd suspicion that no such ostrakon or papyrus will ever emerge."

Widely as in some important respects I presume to differ from Dr. Williams, I am near to him here; for I should say without hesitation that, were it clearly demonstrated that Jesus Christ never existed, or that He was not that divine-human Being which the New Testament represents, the catholic faith of Christendom would be proved a great delusion, and, having lost my hope for time and for eternity, I should look round for some theosophy or "natural religion" to be for me its little availing substitute.

Any statement of the faith that a man may attempt to-day must of necessity be a restatement. To be valid or genuine it must be in truth a restatement of what Dr. N. P. Williams calls "the fundamental Deposit of the faith." The definition of this "fundamental Deposit" is the purpose of this book. I am not concerned to expound my own religious opinions, but rather that faith which is declared in Scripture and is variously defined in the creeds and Confessions of the Church. I have become somewhat impatient of those who regard "orthodox" as a term of abuse, as if no thinking man could profess the same faith as his fathers. But is the old faith really indistinguishable from the old theological formulations of it? I do not forget the ancient saying that a man may hold the catholic faith in a heretical spirit, or he may hold an heretical faith in the catholic spirit; but I cannot think it a light matter to "err concerning the faith," and in this book I am attempting to define that ultimate faith which if a man deny he may not claim, so far as his thought is concerned, to be a Christian.

In spite, however, of what I hope is the orthodoxy as well as the dogmatism of this book, I trust that it may serve an eirenical purpose. In Protestantism at the present time, and not least in that branch of it to which I adhere, there is serious danger of a split between "catholics" and "modernists," or "dogmatists" and "nebulists." A split there may have to be, for between those who hold and those who do not hold that the Church has been entrusted with a final apostolic Gospel there is so deep a cleavage of thought that I see only danger in attempting to combine both views in one religious organization. But the division which I would help to overcome is between those who use and treasure the old formulæ of the faith and those who, through intellectual honesty, cannot employ the old language and repudiate many of the old ideas, yet desire with all their hearts to restate the eternal Gospel in the language of the day.

I suspect that in the future, as in the past, I must suffer the contradictory reproaches of being too radical and too traditional. But it will, I hope, be granted that I am offering not a mere compromise between the old and the new, but a theological principle which is self-consistent, intelligible, and weighty.

It may be agreed that, unless Protestantism can find some such principle, its disintegration must come soon. The hope for the future lies in a true catholicism. Protestantism as a whole, and each of the sects into which it is now divided, must look back to its early fathers with veneration and with thanks to Almighty God. But the day for sectarianism has gone by ; and if the Reformation was, as I believe, a glorious rediscovery of the essential Gospel, we should clearly recognize that the great schism, which attended it, was sheer tragedy. But what is the true principle of unity and catholicity ? Is it the Word or is it the hierarchy ? In theological terms my book may be described as an attempt to define and expound the catholicism of the Word which is the fundamental principle of Protestantism. But I conceive that this principle will be not unintelligible to Roman Catholics, as I hope it may serve to meet the present urgent spiritual and intellectual need of Protestants.

It may well be true, as Dr. Ambrosius Czakó argues, that the theology of a Church is the reflection or projection of its inner life and worship ; in this case we may expect as many theologies as there are divergencies of Church-life. It would, however, be a gross misconceiving of my purpose, and a signal mark of my failure, if a critic should say that my book presents what a Congregationalist or even a Protestant conceives to be the substance of the Christian faith. I write, of course, as a Protestant, for it is I that write; but since my purpose is to define what is the common or catholic faith of Christendom, I am as much concerned with the faith of Roman Catholics as with the faith of the great mediæval Church which is the mother of us all. I believe that we best serve the Great Church as we serve faithfully that branch of it in which we have been placed, but it is permitted to us, wherever we be, to chafe at the limitations imposed upon us by the divisions of the Church, and to love where we cannot at present share. My own personal position in regard to these matters is a feeling of much kinship with Sir Thomas Browne, when he writes:

"To be particular, I am of that Reformed new-cast Religion, wherein I dislike nothing but the Name; of the same belief our Saviour taught, the Apostles disseminated, the Fathers authorized, and the Martyrs confirmed. . . . Yet I have not so shaken hands with those desperate Resolutions, who had rather venture at large their decayed bottom than bring her in to be new trimmed in the Dock . . . as to stand in Diameter and Sword's point with them: We have reformed from them, not against them; for (omitting those Improperations and Terms of Scurrility betwixt us, which only difference our affections and not our cause), there is between us one common Name and Appellation, one Faith and necessary body of Principles common to us both; and therefore I am not scrupulous to converse and live with them, to enter their Churches in defect of ours, and either pray with them or for them. . . . Holy-water and Crucifix (dangerous to the common people) deceive not my judgment nor abuse my devotion at all: I am, I confess, naturally inclined to that which misguided Zeal terms Superstition: my common conversation I do acknowledge austere, my behaviour full of rigour, sometimes not without morosity; yet at my Devotion I love to use the civility of my knee, my hat, and hand, with all those outward and sensible motions which may express or promote my invisible Devotion. I should violate my own arm rather than a Church, nor willingly deface the name of Saint or Martyr. At the sight of a Cross or Crucifix I can dispense with my hat, but scarce with the thought or memory of my Saviour. . . . I could never hear the *Ave-Mary* Bell without an elevation, or think it a sufficient warrant, because they erred in one circumstance, for me to err in all."

It becomes us to be catholics before we are Protestants or Romanists, and Protestants before we are adherents of our particular persuasions.

One more point must be made clear. My purpose in this book is to define the faith, not to defend it, still less to offer a judgment as to who is and who is not a Christian. I doubt not that, as many have fallen into grievous reproach in matters of morality without forfeiting the name of true believers, so many have erred grievously concerning the faith who yet are Christ's by love and loyalty. So, too, with respect to the faith, the method and order of exposition differ from the method and order of appropriation. Dogmatics begins when the journey to Christ is accomplished; it starts, as I shall indicate, from the "divinity" of Jesus Christ; but the faith itself in His "divinity" will start normally from His humanity. Thus in his book *The Son of God* (which with Professor Dodd's *Parables of the Kingdom* I would commend to all my readers), Professor Karl Adam says: "The road to the *mysterium Christi* leads not across the uncontrollable secret places of the transcendental, past the precipices of the paradoxical and incredible, but over the bright open plain of the historical life of Jesus. This is the way of the faith, *per Jesum ad Christum* or, more plainly with St. Augustine, *per hominem Christum tendis ad Deum Christum.*" My book is not offered as a substitute for the study of the Gospels.

Professor Dodd's book, *The Apostolic Preaching*, appeared after all my proofs were corrected. My book may not improperly be described as an attempt to work out the theological implications of his exposition of the Gospel in the New Testament. I could wish that his book might be read before mine, and mine be judged in the light of his.

My grateful thanks are due to my friend, the Rev. John Wilding, B.A., of Newbury, Berks, for the index which he has generously prepared.

Part I

THE NATURE OF DOGMA

CHAPTER I

HOW IS THE FAITH TO BE DEFINED?

By the lowest common factor?

HOW is the Christian faith to be defined?

The Christian faith, of course, is that which the Christians profess. But obviously it will not suffice to ask any chance Christian what are his beliefs and to assume that we are receiving in answer a proper definition of the faith; for many Christians have a very defective grasp upon their principles. And, indeed, who are the Christians whom we might interrogate? Are we to include the Christian Scientists among them, or those Unitarians who claim the Christian name? Even if it were possible to define all Christians in advance, and discover the lowest common factor of belief shared by all, our answer would be unsatisfactory. The attempt to find the minimum of faith, and to ascertain the point at which the half-believer becomes an unbeliever, is a depressing pursuit. It behoves us rather to know the undistorted creed which all Christians are endeavouring to apprehend.

By the creeds?

A more satisfactory answer to our question would be gained by reference to the very noteworthy agreement of the leaders of the Churches reached at the Lausanne Conference in 1927; it runs thus: "Notwithstanding the differences of doctrine among us, we are united in a common Christian Faith which is proclaimed in the Holy Scriptures and is witnessed to and safeguarded in the Œcumenical Creed, commonly called the Nicene, and in the Apostles' Creed, which Faith is continuously confirmed in the spiritual experience of the Church of Christ."

For my present purpose, however, even this answer is unsatisfactory. There must be very many Protestants who have never read, much less recited, the creeds (for their convenience I have added them as an appendix to this book), and who would certainly not sign them as an accurate summary of their personal beliefs. The creeds are, indeed, part of the precious inheritance of œcumenical Christianity, but we are asking, What exactly is that Christian faith to which the creeds bear witness and which they safeguard? Is the faith to be simply identified with the creeds? And, if so, how are the creeds to be interpreted? Thus, for instance, the Apostles' Creed declares that our Lord "descended into hell." Are we to take this literally on peril of denying the faith? Or may we take it symbolically, and, if so, what does it symbolize? Or may we say that, since this clause does not appear in the old Roman creed from which the Apostles' Creed was evolved, nor in the Nicene Creed, it cannot be essential to the faith? Or, again, the Nicene Creed asserts that our Lord is "of one substance with the Father." What does this mean in modern speech? Is it a theological proposition correct within the limits of ancient thought, but unnecessary or inapposite in terms of our philosophies? I intend to prefer an answer to these questions; enough for the moment that the creeds themselves need explanation, and are, therefore, rather the symbols of our problem than the answer to it.

It is important here to draw a distinction which may be indicated by an illustration. The creeds are formulations of the Christian faith in God as Father, Son, and Holy Spirit. One man will say: "I do not deny the Christian doctrine of the Trinity, but that doctrine is expressed in language which to-day is almost meaningless. Had I lived in the fourth century, I am prepared to believe that this doctrine would have been the best available expression of my faith, but it does not express my faith to-day. I will attempt to the best of my ability to retranslate the old doctrine into terms which have some meaning for me. Ultimately, I suppose, I believe what the old formulæ sought to express; but if you present me with the old terms, and ask me whether that is what I believe, I must say No." Another will say: "I am a Christian, and the Fathers who produced the old Trinitarian formulæ were Christians; therefore I suppose that ultimately we must mean the same thing, but frankly I do not believe the old doctrine; indeed, I regard it as a definite misrepresentation of the Christian religion, and I reject it." These two positions are distinguishable, but are they finally distinct? The first speaker says, in effect, that the language of the ancient faith is so inadequate or antiquated that he cannot honestly adopt it as his own, though he must seek to reinterpret it. The latter rejects the doctrine, but claims that he does not cease thereby to be a Christian; though his restatement of the faith bear no relation to the old formulæ, ultimately, he believes, it is the same faith in both cases. Is this a difference in degree, or a difference in kind? Is the former a Christian believer because he accepts the substance (though not the formulation) of the old faith, while the latter is no Christian because he rejects a fundamental dogma?

This is a problem as perplexing as it is unavoidable. For scholars the most satisfying formulation of the Trinitarian faith is the so-called Athanasian Creed; but if we ask the ordinary Christian whether the Athanasian

Creed expresses his personal faith, he will be hard put to it to answer Yes. We must, then, seek to ascertain whether he actually repudiates the truth enunciated by the creed, or fails to see that the creed is implicit in what he actually believes, or denies the creed only because he misinterprets it.

It is quite obvious, then, that our question, " What exactly is the Christian faith ? " is not satisfactorily answered by a recitation of the creeds, for the creeds may be explained, or explained away, or innocently misinterpreted in various ways. If it be replied that the creeds accurately define the Christian faith if they be interpreted in the sense in which they were originally intended, we may possibly have an answer that is satisfactory to scholars, but we have no useful answer whatever to the modern man's question, " What exactly is the Christian faith in terms that I can understand ? "

What we need in respect of the creeds is a principle whereby to distinguish form from content, so that we may know whether or not a hesitancy about particular phrases implies a doubt concerning the faith itself. We need a definition of that " common Christian Faith " which, as the Lausanne Conference declared, " is witnessed to and safeguarded in " the creeds. In other words, how can we restate the faith if we are not able to distinguish form from substance in that which has to be restated? But our definition of the faith to be restated, if it be not the creeds themselves, must itself be a restatement. Therefore, it appears, we must either be unable to define the substance of that which has to be restated, or else we must argue in a circle. What possible escape is there from this dilemma ?

There is a certain scrupulosity of the tortuous intellect that is best regarded as a disease. I shall maintain that it is possible for human beings to convey clear and intelligible meaning even though language be always more or less inadequate to thought, and that we can define the Christian faith even though we can never define it perfectly or finally.

But, before we consider this, we may look at another possible answer to our question. As we have seen, we cannot accept as a satisfactory definition of the faith the religious opinions of any chance Christian; for his grasp upon Christian truth may be defective. Nor can we be satisfied with that minimum belief which all deemed to be Christians hold in common; for if I want to know what is the faith of the Conservative Party, I do not want to be told the opinions of the man who is so poor a Conservative that he is on the brink of joining "Labour." Nor is our need met by a recitation of the creeds, for our question might as well have been couched in the form, What exactly is that faith to which the creeds bear witness?

By the faith of outstanding Christians?

But we might take a number of outstanding Christians of different periods and different types and assume that their common faith, when we have extracted and defined it, will be the answer to our question. Surely St. Augustine and St. Bernard and St. Francis of Assisi and Luther and Wesley and General Booth and Cardinal Newman and Bishop Gore and Albert Schweitzer have held the Christian faith? All we have to do, therefore, is to ascertain and set down that which they have held in common. But this method will not help us. These men, indeed, are all indubitably Christians, but are they all orthodox Christians? We cannot answer the question until first we have decided upon what is orthodoxy, and, when that is decided, we shall know, without further enquiry, what is the Christian faith.

The theologian's starting-point

The most difficult question for the theologian would seem to be his starting-point. How can he move forward with confidence till he can define that faith which it is his business to expound? As an urgent and seriously perplexing problem this question is distinctively modern. When St. John of Damascus wrote his first great treatise on systematic theology, his task was simply to expound the creeds which were couched in the current language of his age. It was his task to work out the implications of the creeds, but not to restate the Christian faith by translation into another idiom. When St. Thomas gathered up the wisdom of the ancient world and systematized Christian theology in the thirteenth century, he may be said to have translated theology into the idiom of Aristotle, but he had no doubt as to the substance of the faith to be so translated. When John Calvin wrote the first systematic treatise on Protestant dogmatics, he rewrote theology from a new point of view, but the creeds he never questioned. He had no hesitations about such insistent modern questions as whether the doctrine of the Trinity is integral to Christianity, whether God really became man, whether a Christian must believe in the Virgin Birth and the physical Resurrection. The question of the definition of the Christian faith is to-day raised in so radical a form as to be virtually a new question.

The test of reason

We may distinguish four answers that are offered at the present time. First, there are those who say that every alleged item of the Christian creed must be tested at the bar of reason. To this principle, if it be rightly interpreted, no exception can be taken. Our reason is given us by God that we may understand, and faith cannot contradict reason; therefore, it is argued, whatsoever does not commend itself to reason cannot be of faith.

This asseveration of reason is to be welcomed as a protest against those who would reduce the Christian faith to some sort of incommunicable and esoteric experience or to a series of mere value-judgments impressive to one and uncongenial to another. Protestantism has been far too ready to retreat from the battlefield where only rigorous logic can avail; but this principle that faith must be brought to the test of reason is used to cover two totally different conceptions.

The Christian faith must be logically coherent; it must not involve any internal contradiction, nor be inconsistent with any truth that we know by the light of reason; we may even demand that it offer us the key to unlock the whole mystery of life and of the world; there must be nothing to which it is not relevant. So far we may agree. But if a man say, "Prove to me, by strict and unanswerable logic, that the Deity is three 'Persons' in one God, that Jesus Christ is the eternal Son of God, that He died for our sins and rose for our justification; then, and then only, will I regard the Christian faith as worthy of the acceptance of a thinking man"–we must answer that we are men, not God, that our human reason has human limitations, that here we see but through a glass darkly, and that we do not make the outrageous claim to solve the riddle of the universe as we solve a problem in mathematics. It is indubitably right to claim that the Christian faith must be *tested* by reason, but it cannot be *given* by reason as the conclusion of a syllogism or the answer of a sum. When we ask whether the Christian faith is credible, we must test it by the light of reason; when we ask what the Christian faith *is*, we cannot get our answer by consulting books on philosophy or logic. In a word, the Christian faith is what it is, not what any modern rationalism may think it ought to be. Reason, therefore, by itself will not yield us the definition that we want.

The test of experience

The second modern answer to our search for a definition of the substance of the faith is in terms of religious experience. As marking a reaction from arid, speculative, and purely academic dogmatisms this contention may be welcomed. That which is not related in some way to personal, inward apprehension can scarcely be of faith. But this principle, like that of reason, is made to cover two quite different conceptions. It is one thing to say: "Philosophies change, and theological systems vary, but, as the hymns and prayers of the Universal Church make manifest, there is one fundamental religious experience which Augustinian and Thomist, Calvinist and Arminian express in their varying idioms. Therefore, once I have apprehended this religious experience, I am in possession of the substance of the Christian faith in distinction from its various forms." It is quite another thing to say, as some are apt to do to-day: "I claim to be a Christian, but anything in the traditional Christian faith which does not correspond with my private religious experience I am free to reject as no part of the substance of the faith." This latter position, which virtually assumes that the Christian faith is whatever I happen to believe, can hardly be maintained by any when it is baldly stated, but it is often unconsciously assumed by individuals and groups who would make their own religious experience the test of truth or of the Christian faith.

The view that the substance of the Christian faith must correspond with that profound religious experience to which the saints of all ages and all branches of the Church bear witness is true and fruitful. Faith and religious experience must go hand in hand. *Veritatem videre est eam habere – et quodammodo esse.* We may welcome, therefore, this principle of experience, but of itself it will not go far to elucidate our question. For the term " experience " itself needs much further analysis. Thus it is an uncontradicted Christian doctrine, accepted by every branch of the Christian Church, that in the beginning God created the heavens and the earth, yet obviously the creation of the world cannot have been the direct religious or historical " experience " of any human being. In what sense, then, may we say that Christian doctrine corresponds with the experience of Christians?

Still, it is doubtless true that, if we could apprehend the classical or typical and ever-recurring religious experience of the saints to which the prayers and praises not less than the theologies of the Church bear witness, we should be grasping the very core and substance of the Christian faith. The reference to experience, therefore, gives us a valuable pointer, but beyond that it does not help us greatly. The religious experience of the saints is not a blank experience; it has intellectual content; it is expressed in the creeds, hymns, and theologies of Christendom. When we have expressed it in our own terms, we shall have restated for our day the substance of the Christian faith. This is precisely our task. Religious experience, then, like reason, offers us a test of doctrine but does not of itself yield us the doctrine.

The answer of the Fundamentalists

The third modern answer to our question is offered by the so-called Fundamentalists. Taking their stand upon the traditional Christian doctrine that the Bible is God's Holy Word they tell us that we shall understand the substance of the Christian faith, not by considering the dictates of human reason, nor by arguing from the varying experiences of imperfectly religious men, but by studying the objective revelation vouchsafed to us in Scripture. The great strength of the Fundamentalist position is that in the Bible it offers us an objective norm which has always, or till very recently, been accepted by all Christians. Its weakness is that " the devil can quote Scripture to his purpose," or, in other words, that we need not merely the Scriptures but some principle of exegesis by which we may interpret the very manifold data of the Scriptures. In practice the Fundamentalists interpret the Bible along the lines of traditional Protestant theology, as the Roman Catholics interpret it along the lines of their accepted doctrine. Therefore the Fundamentalists in fact use Scripture rather as the support than as the basis of their theology. They tend, therefore, to ascribe to their theology the same sort of absolute validity which others ascribe to the historic creeds. They give us little or no help in our attempt to distinguish form from content in the Christian faith.

The answer of the Roman Church

The fourth answer to our question is that of Rome. The Roman Church declares that the faithful must accept not merely the creeds but all authoritative definitions of doctrine literally and verbally. It does not deny that there is, or may be, a distinction between form and content in doctrine ; thus clearly such Jewish terms as " Messiah " or " kingdom of heaven " must be translated into terms comprehensible to the Gentile world, and in this sense there has been doctrinal development ; but, once the Church has formally defined a doctrine, this definition must be accepted as it stands ; further, since every doctrine so defined is reckoned a truth of revelation vouchsafed by God, the distinction between form and content vanishes. No Roman Catholic, for instance, may say: " I reject the doctrine of the Immaculate Conception as formulated by authority, but I believe the fundamental truth which I suppose that doctrine to represent, therefore I believe the doctrine."

Thus Rome presents to the world an attitude of unqualified rigidity. For practical purposes, and for popular propaganda, she recognizes no distinction between substance and form in Christian truth, but, if we cross-question her theologians, the matter is not so clear. Thus all human language is relative; no description is wholly adequate to fact; truth can only be set forth in imperfect human terms. The French Modernist le Roy says: " If dogmas formulated absolute truth in adequate terms . . . they would be unintelligible to us. If they only gave an imperfect truth, relative and changing, their imposition could not be legitimate." Not only do Roman Catholic theologians recognize the difficulty here, but they are, in principle, bound to give weight to it through their fundamental conception that human language concerning divine things must from the nature of the case be either negative or analogical.

Accordingly Professor Karl Adam sets out to explain " why it is that the ideal cannot be realized in this world." He writes: " The first and most obvious cause of these conflicts lies in the very nature of revelation, just because divine truth and grace are therein conveyed to us in earthly vessels. God's revelation makes use of human instruments, the infinite of the finite; the ineffable and transcendent is clothed in visible forms and signs. Two distinct factors here impinge on each other, factors which of their nature cannot be simply assimilated the one to the other, but can only achieve a relation of similarity, a relation of analogy. . . . So that no assertion that we make about God is an exhaustive assertion. It contains truth, but not the whole truth, and therefore possesses only an analogous value. . . . All our names for God are but ' shy gestures, which would gladly approach God nearer and yet can only greet Him from afar.' But even God's supernatural revelation, even all those truths which go beyond the data of nature and are directly taught us by divine revelation, especially through God's revelation in His Son, do not enter our consciousness in their original nature and in their self-evident force and immediacy, but are mediated through human conceptions and notions. The dogmas, in which these supernatural truths have been authoritatively formulated by the Church, denote the Absolute, but are not themselves the Absolute. The conceptual forms in which they are stated belong to specific periods of time, being borrowed mostly from Greek philosophy, and express the supernatural truths truly and aptly and in a form intelligible in every age, but by no means exhaustively or perfectly. ' We see now as in a mirror, in a dark manner.' These words of St. Paul hold true of all supernatural knowledge." There is a " permanently enigmatical character of the truths of our faith." Once more, " the eternal light of revelation is differently reflected in the prism of each age, with different angles of refraction. The supernatural reality is not manifested in naked truth, as it is in itself, but enters into the particular age and therefore in a form determined by that age. In this way it becomes an enkindling and fruitful and present force ; but at the same time it loses in the process something of the austerity and majesty of its supernatural being. It suffers a sort of ' emptying ' (κένωσις), it despoils itself, and takes the form of a slave, as the Divine Word despoiled Himself when He became man."

The matter could scarcely be better put. We may say, then, that the Roman Church is deeply aware of the problem ; but, alas ! it has at present done little to solve it or even to make it realized. The language of Greek philosophy used in dogmatic definitions, we are told, is intelligible in every age, but no definition is exhaustive or even perfect, and, indeed, there is a " permanently enigmatical " element in all the pronouncements of faith. If we ask a Roman Catholic, " What exactly is the Christian faith ? " he will give us an exact answer in the language of another age ; when we ask, " What is the substance of the Christian faith in the language of to-day ? " he can only give us such documents as the creeds, which, as we have seen, are inadequate for our purpose.

The faith neither indefinite nor fully definable

What exactly is the Christian faith ? The question may be inevitable and yet unanswerable. Most certainly the Christian faith is not indefinite, yet from the nature of the case it can never be perfectly and finally defined. Whatever form of words we propose, there will always be some Christians who will say, " We cannot accept the Christian faith in precisely these terms." There must be a distinction between substance and form, but we can never define the substance except in some form from which ideally it must be distinct ; hence the attempt to find any particular form of words which will be universally accepted by Christians as a complete, final, and undistorted representation of the faith is the pursuit of the unattainable. None the less, provided that we refuse the diseased isolation of solipsism, we must agree that propositions can convey definite meaning, that we can say what we mean, even though we can never say all that we mean, nor can our language (except in mathematics) be wholly adequate to our thought. It must be possible to state – that is, to restate – the Christian faith in the language of to-day, and to test the adequacy of our restatement by considering its true equivalence with the statements of yesterday which we are capable of understanding in their ancient form.

The task of translation

The task of restatement may be immensely difficult, but it is both possible and necessary. It can never be finally achieved, and it cannot be achieved at all by amateurs. It is a form of the wider problem of translation in general from one language to another. Thus not Pope, nor T. E. Lawrence, nor Lang, Leaf, and Myers, can give a perfect English equivalent of Homer, but Homer can be so translated into English that the man who knows no Greek may have a real understanding of the poet, and, indeed, an English poet with a translation may understand Homer better than a pedantic linguist. Ideally a poem may even gain by the process of translation. Omar Khayyám was by general consent most fortunate in his English sponsor, and many admirers of Professor Gilbert Murray may judge that some fragments of Euripides gain more than they lose as they issue from his mind in English dress.

It is to be supposed that the sayings of our Lord were uttered and remembered first in Aramaic. Some scent of the soil, some subtlety of connotation, must inevitably be lost when they suffered translation into the Greek of our New Testaments. Again, those who read the Gospels in Wyclif's translation must feel that in some strange way the Gospels are acclimatized in mediæval England. There is gain in familiarity and homeliness where there is loss in accuracy. From this kind of relativity there can be no deliverance in this world.

But, in respect of formal doctrine, it may be, and has been, maintained that translation may bring far more gain than loss. Thus when Christianity issued from the womb of Judaism, the term "Messiah" or "Christ" was no longer fully intelligible. The Greek term "Logos," which came to be used to express the significance of our Lord, is in no sense a direct translation of "Messiah," but few would deny that philosophically it is more adequate. Later the term "substance" was adopted into the creed, in spite of protests that it was not Biblical. Dr. N. P. Williams thinks that there is something final about this category; Dr. Karl Adam seems to claim only that it is permanently intelligible; many modernists wish to find some more personal substitute. In any case this term "substance" is a good instance of the translation of the faith of the Bible into another idiom of thought. Our task, as retranslators, is to find some modern equivalent for the old phraseology or, if possible, some category which is more adequate than that which the Nicene Fathers knew. But, of course, this can only be done by those who really understand what the old theologians meant. I venture to stress this obvious point because many who, to their credit, are deeply concerned with the duty of restating theological terms are far too impatient to ascertain whether their own proposals are any real equivalent of that which they are intended to replace.

The task of retranslating the Christian faith into modern terms in the form of a new systematic theology, such as St. Thomas and Calvin and Schleiermacher accomplished for their generations, is a task wholly beyond my reach, and I hope it will be plain that I do not conceive myself to be attempting it. My purpose is more modest. It is to indicate, in language that will be intelligible, and with reference to a principle of the farthest application, what elements in the traditional theology and religious language of Christendom must be deemed of the substance of the faith, however they be retranslated, and what elements pertain to the form which may be transient.

Only possible within the Church

This is a task which can only be attempted from within the Christian Church. A man must hold the catholic faith before he can interpret or retranslate it. A writer must offer his credentials. My own position, then, is this: when I read St. John of Damascus or St. Thomas Aquinas or John Calvin – to take the pre-eminent exponents of the theology of East, of West, and of Protestantism – my mind is often unpersuaded in detail, but to the whole my heart consents; some of their arguments I find it hard to follow, some of their positions I could not accept; but fundamentally, and in substance, I know that theirs is the same faith as that into which I was baptized, and by which I live. I could not make all their words my own; much, as I realize, I should wish, if I could, to express in different terms, but fundamentally I in my small way believe that which in their large way, and in the language of their day, they have expressed. It is their faith and not another that I would set forth. It is this vivid sense of fundamental unity with the past in one faith and one Church which alone could justify me in attempting the task with which I am here concerned. But it is strictly necessary that I should indicate some objective principle by which I may know that I am not merely an eclectic picker and chooser, taking from the past what appeals to me, and rejecting what I do not relish, but rather am in measure able to distinguish form from content in the faith.

It will be agreed that the Christian faith corresponds with the Christian revelation. Next, therefore, we will consider the nature of revelation.

CHAPTER II

REVELATION

I

THE term " revelation " is used in various senses. When some new fact is discovered by a scientist, the event has two sides ; it may be represented as man's discovery or as God's " revelation." When we speak of the Christian " revelation," we use the term in a narrower or, at least, a different sense.

Definition of the term

In another use of the term all religion is of revelation. In different ways and in different respects, apart altogether from Judaism and Christianity, God has made Himself known to men. There was a time when Christians regarded all non-Christian religion as the devil's work ; we have now happily reverted to the Biblical and early Christian conviction that God has not left Himself without witness among any nation. It is, therefore, quite proper to speak of revelation in connection with Zoroaster and Socrates and Plato, and even with reference to the religious apprehensions of primitive peoples. There is, further, the great field of " natural religion " – by which is meant a religion of reason based on such ideas as God, freedom, and immortality, which man is supposed to achieve without any " special revelation." In this sense natural religion, or the religion " of the plain man," or non-supernatural religion, is often contrasted with the religions that claim to be based on " revelation." There is a real distinction ; none the less, as no man can know his friend apart from self-revelation on the friend's part, so no man can have any religious knowledge of God, unless God be pleased to reveal Himself. From this point of view all religion is of revelation. But the revelation which is correlative to man's discoveries by the exercise of his reason is distinguished from revelation in the dogmatic sense or in the special sense in which Christianity, for instance, claims to be a religion of revelation.

Natural and Revealed Religion

This more special or theological sense of the term is thus described by a Roman Catholic divine: "Revelation in the theological sense is the imparting of religious truths to men by God, either directly or through an angel. The distinguishing mark of revelation lies in this, that God manifests Himself immediately, not only mediately through His handiwork as in Creation and in world-events, though these, too, manifest God's actuality and Being and hence are also called *natural* revelation. In distinction from this, revelation in the strict sense of the word bears a supernatural character."

This definition will serve for the moment. A distinction is drawn between ordinary and special, or between natural and supernatural, revelation. Is this distinction ultimate and fundamental?

Archbishop Temple answers No. "What is needed," he says in his Gifford Lectures, "and what is plainly coming to pass before our eyes, is the deliberate and total repudiation of any distinction of spheres as belonging respectively to Natural and Revealed Religion or Theology." This needs some explanation. In old days it was maintained that certain truths about God – as that He exists; that He is Creator; that He is the providential Disposer of this world's affairs – might be known by the light of natural reason, but that certain further truths concerning Him – as that He is three Persons in one God; that He is incarnate in Jesus Christ; that He has redeemed us "by the blood of the Cross" – could only be made known by supernatural revelation to the eye of faith, and could never be discovered by man's natural reason.

This view of revelation might be denied on either of two grounds; it might be said that God does not reveal "truths" or doctrines at all, but reveals Himself or "values," or even (apparently) spiritual states. Or it might be said that the truths of Christianity, such as the Trinity, the Divinity of Christ, and the Atonement, can be discovered or realized in precisely the same way as any other spiritual truths. Again, the denial of a distinction between Natural and Revealed religion might mean either the denial of supernatural religion altogether or merely the denial that any truths are to be accepted on bare authority. The answer here given to this question will appear from the discussion that follows. Enough for the moment that, if for the rest we confine our attention exclusively to the Christian faith or Christian revelation, it is not with any suggestion that there is no knowledge of God apart from Christianity. "Every true saying, whoever be its author," says St. Ambrose, "is from the Holy Spirit."

Doctrine is of human construction

Revelation, says the Roman theologian quoted above, is "the imparting of religious truths." This corresponds with the customary phrase, "truths of revelation." That which is revealed, it appears, is truth or truths. How is this possible? If truth is as God imparts it, it must be absolute in form, for God cannot be thought to impart to man that which is imperfectly or but approximately true. But truths must be imparted in intellectual terms intelligible to human beings. But le Roy is unquestionably right in his assertion that "if dogmas formulated absolute truth in adequate terms . . . they would be unintelligible to us." The great theologians, not least those honoured by the Roman Church, insist upon the weakness and limitations of human mental powers. We are not capable of receiving absolute truth, but only such truth as can be expressed in human language which is imperfect and relative. God must become flesh, and truth must be expressed, and therefore imperfectly represented, in human language if we are to understand. We must distinguish between divine truth and man's intellectual formulation of it. We may believe that the Holy Spirit has guided the Church in the construction of doctrine, but there can be no dispute that dogma or doctrine is of human construction. The dogmas of the Church, as Professor Karl Adam says, "denote the Absolute, but are not themselves the Absolute"—ἄρρητον καὶ ἀκατάληπτον τὸ θεῖον.

It is Himself whom God reveals

Therefore we must say that truths are revealed in a secondary sense; they are rather the intellectual formulation of revelation than revelation itself. Strictly, the subject and object of revelation are one. It is God who reveals, and it is Himself whom He reveals. God, we say, has revealed Himself to us in Jesus Christ; Christian doctrine, therefore, is the intellectual expression of this revelation of Himself.

Revelation mediated

But, again, there is serious difficulty in this conception. We can understand that man may have some sense of God's majesty and power through Creation or through the processes of history, that he may have some inkling of God through his natural reason or through that sense of the sacred which is part of his human constitution; even so, " behold these are but the outskirts of His ways, and how small a whisper do we hear of Him ! " But all such knowledge of God is mediated and indirect. " No man may see God and live." It is claimed that the mystics in their rapture have direct and immediate access to God. This is a matter about which those who are not mystics may not lightly dogmatize. But, if the natural eye of man cannot gaze upon the sun without destruction, nor can see the ultra-violet or infra-red rays of light, how much more is the eye of the soul incapable of seeing very God Himself, whose Being passes thought or imagination! We may speak of seeing God in things or persons, but we may not with propriety speak of seeing God Himself.

The Christian as much as any other is a mediated revelation. We see God in Christ, the Mediator between God and man. The Christian revelation, then, is that which comes to us through Christ. But if all revelation is the self-unveiling of God, all revelation in every religion must be homogeneous, and it does not appear how the Christian revelation can differ in kind, but only in content, from all other revelations.

The Incarnation the distinctive revelation

Yet a distinction is undoubtedly asserted in the Christian faith. It is admitted that God has revealed something of Himself to prophets, seers, philosophers, and poets, not in Judaism only, but throughout the pagan world. He *spoke* to the prophets, but in His Son He *came*.

It must be borne in mind that I am not attempting an essay in the philosophy of religion, nor in apologetics. It is no part of my present task to defend the Christian faith or to attempt to show that it is true. I am seeking only to define, as precisely as may be, what it is. Christians have maintained as of the very essence of their faith that Jesus Christ is in some sense God Himself incarnate.

Thus the revelation of God in Christ is different in kind from every other revelation.

The conception of Incarnation, taken seriously, implies that God was amongst men in some sort of incognito. There was a purely human, a wholly historical, side to the life of Jesus Christ. Not all men " beheld His glory," and even believers beheld that glory through, and in, the human and historical. We here meet with the central mystery of the faith, which Christians can state but not explain ; we are here, as I suppose, at the watershed where the catholic faith of Christendom divides from those many christianized philosophies which offer themselves as substitutes for, or even as restatements of, the Christian faith.

The Incarnation may be explained away as a mere metaphor. The sayings of Christ and His deeds of mercy may be represented as the reflection or counterpart of the wisdom and goodness of God, so that Christ may be conceived as the undistorting mirror of the Father's likeness ; as such, He is not only Lord of the prophets, but in some sense divine.

I do not wish to write slightingly of this point of view, but three comments will be in place. First, the revelation of God in Christ implied here is superior in quality and perfection to the revelation through the prophets, but not different in kind. Second, it is one thing to say that a man on earth mirrors the glory of heaven, it is another thing to say that heaven is come down to earth ; it is one thing to say, God has taught us the truth about Himself in Jesus Christ, another thing to say, He has come Himself to seek and save ; it is one thing to say, Jesus Christ is like God, another to say He is of one substance with God. I do not wish to draw a distinction unfairly sharp, for the two views may be made to approximate, and many, as I suppose, are attempting to express the traditional view in terms of the other, but in the end there is an ultimate distinction between a God-inspired man and God Himself made flesh (between ἄνθρωπος θεοφόρος and θεὸς σεσαρκωμένος). Third, from a theological point of view, if we take " original sin " seriously, it will be found that the conception of an undistorting reflection raises as serious difficulties as the conception of Incarnation. I must return to the christological question later ; meanwhile we note at least a clear *prima facie* distinction between a man like God and God made man, and enquire what the traditional view implies in the matter of revelation.

To put the difference in brief, the view that Jesus Christ is the mirror or reflection of God puts the revelation in abstract terms of the qualities of God – His mercy, His righteousness, His love. The classical or traditional faith sees the revelation of God rather in action than in abstract or general truth.

II

The evidence of the Gospels

It is necessary here to turn aside to Scriptural exegesis. No Christian denies that the teaching of Christ represents the heavenly wisdom, nor that Christ's deeds of mercy express the mercy of the Father, nor that His death on Calvary is the manifestation of the love of God. But if we are content thus to sum up the significance of Jesus Christ, we most seriously distort the picture of Him in the Gospels. The modern scientific and literary criticism of the Gospels began in an age that was so wholly dominated by a dogmatic conception of the Person of Christ that His humanity was recognized only in theory. By a natural reaction from this, and through a somewhat uncritical use of its own tools, criticism at first presented an almost entirely humanized picture of the Saviour. The studies of Dr. Albert Schweitzer, however far his own construction may be from acceptance, have at least destroyed the rationalized and conventionalized portrait of Christ widely accepted at the end of last century. The so-called "historical Christ" in distinction from "the Christ of faith" must not be said to be dead, for it is now plain that He never lived except in the imagination of theologians. The Figure of the Gospels is now seen to be less like the sage Confucius than like the fire-bringer Prometheus.

Our Lord came into Galilee proclaiming that the hour had struck and the Kingdom was at hand. Amid much that is obscure, it is plain that the Kingdom was a key-note of His thought. It is difficult for us to exercise sufficient historical imagination to realize how exciting was this message. After the long silence of the Prophets, after the long years of waiting, after foreign oppressions, one succeeding another, after bitterness and despair and civil war, at last the promise of the Prophets was to be fulfilled – God Himself would act; He would create all things anew as at the beginning; He would vindicate His righteousness before all the heathen. All the terrific passion of Jewish religion and patriotism gathered round the expectation of the Kingdom. Our Lord identified Himself with this cataclysmic hope, and declared that it was upon the brink of its fulfilment.

He came not merely to announce the Kingdom as John had done; He came to bring it. We are apt to think of His miracles as a perhaps legendary commentary upon His teaching. But, as scholars are now making clear, His teaching was rather a commentary on His works, or, better, both teaching and miracles were equally works in demonstration of the Kingdom. " Whether is it easier to say, Thy sins are forgiven thee, or to say, Take up thy bed and walk ? " The teaching of forgiveness or, rather, the act of forgiving and the healing of the long paralysis constitute, not information about God, but the very act of the living God Himself in the bringing of His Kingdom.

A crucial instance in the Gospels is the controversy about Beelzebub. His enemies accused Him of casting out demons by black magic, by the power of the prince of demons. He answered : " If I by the finger of God cast out demons, without doubt the Kingdom of Heaven is come upon you."

We are apt falsely to distinguish between the first part of His ministry in Galilee, as if it were a time of quiet preaching, from the last Judean episodes which we call the Passion, but might as truly call the Action. A distinction there may be in outward condition but not in purpose ; the campaign might fall into two parts, but it was one campaign. We are wont to suppose that He came to give us the Sermon on the Mount and the Parable of the Prodigal Son ; but His purpose is better expressed in the Collect addressed to Him " whose blessed Son was manifested that He might destroy the works of the devil, and make us sons of God and heirs of eternal life." We may not doubt that both the Parable and the Sermon have been mighty instruments for the routing of the enemy, but we must not put the part for the whole, nor interpret His words as though they were mere doctrine and not the power of God in action. His words are not like a theoretical definition, but like a two-edged sword.

And who was He who, issuing from a humble home in Nazareth, spoke and wrought with such authority? We do not claim to find in the Gospels the developed Christology of later centuries. But the Gospels represent Him as taking to Himself the enigmatic title of Son of Man. It was " one like unto a son of man " who, according to the prophet Daniel, was in the last days to receive the everlasting Kingdom from the Most High on behalf of His saints. We have no good reason for doubt that our Lord took this title for Himself. Even should that be disputed, it is clear that in fact He Himself fulfilled the rôle predicted for the Son of Man. He received the Kingdom; He brought it; He embodied it in His own Person.

That He was truly human, the Church has always in theory asserted. As man He slept in weariness; as man He said: "I thirst." But not as man He said: "I came not to call the righteous but sinners"; "The Son of Man came . . . to give His life a ransom for many"; "Come unto Me, all ye that labour and are heavy laden, and I will give you rest"; "He that receiveth you receiveth Me, and He that receiveth Me receiveth not Me but Him that sent Me"; "Ye may eat and drink at My table in My kingdom"; "This cup is the new covenant in My blood"; "None knoweth the Father save the Son." There is not any one saying at which the critics cannot cavil if they will. If any or every one of these passages be suspect, they still together represent the whole picture of the Gospels. He is set before us throughout as having a "self-consciousness," to use our modern term, which is not that of a fallen man like us; rather, He speaks as the royal Son, the Anointed One, the present Voice of the Eternal.[1]

[1] The substance of the last few pages will be found in a more extended form in my essay in the book *The Defence of Christianity* at present in the press. I have no copy of what I wrote there. If I be found guilty of any verbal repetition, I hope that the Dean of St. Paul's and Messrs. Eyre & Spottiswoode will pardon my inadvertence.

I do not here allege that this is credible as history; I know how hard for us moderns is belief; but suchlike beyond all question is the Figure of the Gospels. We may reject the evidence of the Gospels, but, if we do, it is because we cannot believe, not because we have other and better evidence.

The Kingdom, then, is imminent; God is about to act with His outstretched arm and mighty hand. Just at the moment when, as it appears, His disciples began to understand, and one of them confessed, " Thou art Messiah," He began to tell them that the Son of Man must suffer many things and be rejected and be crucified. Was this because He was disillusioned and saw at last that God was not about to act? The evidence is decisively against this. He rode into the city in humble but royal state; He cleared the traffickers and profiteers from the Temple precincts; in the Temple courts where it stood written in great letters, " Death to the Gentile who enters here," He declared, " My house shall be called a house of prayer for all nations "; at the Last Supper, bequeathing to His disciples His own peace, He inaugurated the New Covenant between God and man, and bade His disciples look forward to the coming Kingdom; He met His shameful death as according to the will of God and in the assurance that He, if He should be lifted up, should draw all men unto Him.

If His temptation in the wilderness symbolizes His first throw with the enemy, the Cross is His death-grapple. The narrative that we call the Passion is the story of His Great Offensive in His battle for the establishing of God's Kingdom. " In His suffering all," says John Chrysostom, " He wrought His great and marvellous work."

I am not here concerned with problems of His Person or of His Atonement, but with an intellectual and personal

A personal decision needed

decision which the reader of the narrative cannot avoid. Was He or was He not the Great Deceiver and the Great Deceived? He said that God would intervene decisively and finally; the Kingdom was at hand. Has God so acted? Is the Kingdom come? The conviction that He was deceived may be toned down by the generous admission that, after all, much that He said is permanently true, and that His influence upon mankind has been good beyond all calculation. That is the judgment of the natural man, of unbelief.

The answer of the Christian faith is clear: the consummation of the Kingdom is not yet (and for that consummation He gave no date), but the Kingdom has come – God has intervened; "He hath visited and hath redeemed His people"; Christ died and rose again; He triumphed over all the powers of sin and death; the power of the enemy in principle is broken; and we that once were sinners and lost have been translated out of darkness into His marvellous light; we have been made sons of God and heirs of eternal life. The Church is the mighty act of God, the firstfruits of redemption.

III

Not truths but action

We are not yet concerned with the theology and dogma that underlie this Christian conviction. But it is necessary to grasp this dynamic conception of the Person and work of Christ in order to apprehend the essential nature of the Christian revelation. We must consider our Lord not merely as uttering profound and eternal truths which theologians may make into a system, but as doing an action of eternal, world-altering significance. In the Gospels we apprehend not so much truths about God as God Himself in action.

We are here in the deepest waters. In what sense may we conceive that we apprehend God Himself in distinction from ideas about Him? How can we think of the changeless God in action? And of what nature must Christian dogma be?

It might appear that the apprehension of God Himself in distinction from ideas about Him is not a distinctively Christian experience. The man who has an eye for beauty or an ear for music is often aware of an infinite and eternal Mind or Being or Spirit through the glories of the sunset or the sound of the sea upon the shore. This may well be regarded as an apprehension or intuition of God Himself in distinction from any formal or definable ideas about Him. But it is not this that the Christian means when He claims to apprehend God Himself in Christ.

The mystery of the Incarnation

Christian religious experience, like all other religious experience, as we have seen, is mediated. In its case, not Nature is the medium, but Christ. Christ, however, as the Christian believes, is in some sense God Himself. Thus God is in some sense mediated by Himself; He is apprehended "in the flesh" which is *His* flesh. This is the mystery of the Incarnation. The revelation is both mediate and immediate; it is mediate in that it is through the historical and external and human; it is immediate in that it is not through anything but God Himself.

The distinction from all other revelation may be illustrated thus: if we are at times aware of God through Nature, most certainly we are aware of Him in and through the "humble and holy men of heart," the saints and heroes of human history. Thus, as many would say, we are supremely aware of Him in and through the man Christ Jesus. The traditional Christian conception, however, corresponds rather with the story of the disciples at

Emmaus. When the stranger joins Himself to them upon their homeward road, their heart burns within them as through the medium of this stranger they receive, as we should say, a profound religious experience; hope revives in them, new ideas quicken them, the faith of Israel becomes real again to them; their hearts are stirred and moved as they contemplate the Redeemer in idea. But in the breaking of the bread they behold the very Redeemer Himself. *It is He!* Or, to take another illustration, a man in dire trouble may say to one who comes to help him: "I know that God sent you to help me; in you and through you I apprehend the mercy and the loving-kindness of God." But it is quite another thing to cry out to the visitor, with Thomas, "My Lord and my God," as it is one thing to say, "He *sent* to help me," and another thing to say, "He *came* to help me." Thus, whether or not we regard the notion as credible, the Christian revelation claims to be immediate in a wholly distinctive sense.

Furthermore, this immediacy is always related to action. When the poet, the artist, the musician, or the seer apprehends God through Nature or history, he always conceives himself to be apprehending that which is already there, though he was not aware of it; the divine is, as it were, permanently available to the apprehender's mental or spiritual effort in apprehending, and this, even though he be very conscious that the stimulus whereby he apprehends comes not from his own inward powers, but from the divine itself. That which he has apprehended, he can in some degree, and according to his gifts, represent in music or painting or poetry or through some other medium of expression; he apprehends that which *is*, that which is eternal, changeless, permanent. This is the revelation of God in Natural Religion. It is not inconsistent with, but is to be clearly distinguished from, the apprehension of God in the historic religions. These latter are Judaism and Christianity, but we may confine our attention here to Christianity. The Christian apprehends God not merely in what He *is*, but also in what He *does* – that is, he apprehends God as the immediate agent in certain events, pre-eminently in that series of events which constitute the coming of our Lord. God *sent* His Son; God *came* in Christ; God *took* our nature – such phrases as these are integral to the expression of the Christian faith. In other words, the revelation can only be expressed by active verbs. The Christian apprehends God not only in His supernatural Being, but in His supernatural action. In other words, the Christian faith is distinguishable from the revelation given in Natural Religion because it is inseparable from miracle.

The faith inseparable from miracle

To us who have received our religion from the Hebrews, but our philosophy from the Greeks, the idea of the living, active God is very difficult. Perhaps the most majestic argument ever enunciated by man is that wherein St. Thomas proves the existence, the eternity, the infinity and perfection of the Deity. We must believe that God is, and that He is changeless. But God who is changeless, it would seem, can neither act nor suffer; for action and suffering mean change. Yet even the vaguest belief in Providence implies that God acts, and, if God be incapable of suffering, it will be hard to call Him God. Philosophy, then, seems to require the immutability and impassibility of God, while personal religion insistently asserts that God's outstretched arm is strong to save and His heart is quick to be entreated. This problem belongs to the philosophy of religion in general, and is, therefore, outside the scope of the present enquiry, but we may note that the Christian's insistence upon miracle intensifies the difficulty.

There is no end to the discussion of the nature of miracle, and a new definition need not be attempted here; for two observations, one exegetical, the other dogmatic, will make clear enough the sense in which miracle is integral to the Christian faith. First, as we have seen, the life, the teaching, and the thought of our Lord gather round the advent of God's Kingdom. That Day of the Lord which is the coming of the Kingdom is always supernaturally conceived; it is not a striking event in the general order of Providence, but a new creation; as the Germans say, it is not the *Wendepunkt* but the *Endepunkt* of human history – that is, it is not a corner where the path wends, but the abyss where the path ends; the coming of the Kingdom is not a turning-point of history, but a new beginning. Second, the Christian faith cannot be expressed except in some such term as, "God sent His Son." However we may try to formulate this and make it intelligible to ourselves, it certainly implies an act of God different in kind from the normal operations of His Providence.

We have now seen what is meant by "revelation" in the specifically Christian sense. We must turn to consider in the light of this the nature of Christian dogma.

CHAPTER III

DOGMA

I

TO some the very notion of dogma is an offence. Our apprehension of truth, they say, is ever deepening ; in the search for truth there can be no finality ; all truth that man attains must of necessity be relative ; as in the natural sciences the partial truths attained by one generation must be discarded in the light of another's increased knowledge, so it must be in religion ; the truth of yesterday is the falsehood of to-day.

Undogmatic Christianity a contradiction

Beyond doubt theology must develop, and the Christian faith must be interpreted anew in every dialect of man. But as some propositions, like the law of contradiction, cannot be superseded (for they lie at the basis of thought itself), so, if it has once been shown that the existence of God is a necessary postulate of thought, the argument must stand true for thought throughout all time. So, too, if it once was true that Christ died for the sins of the whole world, the statement of fact remains true for ever ; the fact abides, however much the interpretation of it may vary in the course of time. Scientific theory develops through the more careful or extensive observation of facts ; but the stars at which the astronomer gazes to-day are the same stars which awed and bewildered our first fathers. If dogma means theoretical explanation, it is, indeed, reasonable to suppose that there will be no element of permanence in it ; but if dogma denote spiritual fact, there is no ground upon which to anticipate its transience. The denial of the permanence of dogma in Christianity presupposes that dogma in religion is parallel to theoretical formulation of law in natural science. The often-drawn parallel between theology and the natural sciences is perilous. Religion is much more closely akin to music and poetry than to the branches of knowledge which deal only with the measurable aspects of the world. The canons of music and criticism, it is true, make no claim to finality, and therefore are not parallel to " the fundamental truths of the Christian religion " ; but, whatever development music and literature may show, no one wisely hopes to be a greater musician than was Bach, a greater poet than was Homer. So, too, no one may claim to be more religious than Jeremiah, more Christian than St. Paul. But some will argue that, just because religion is akin to music or to poetry, there is no proper place for dogma in it.

Hence comes the widespread demand for an " undogmatic Christianity." Christianity, men say, is a life, a spirit, not a creed. As a protest against the rigid dogmatisms, the narrow and unsympathetic orthodoxies, the meticulous tests and heresy hunts of older days this demand for an undogmatic faith is intelligible. But it must be amended before it will make sense. For those who plead for an undogmatic faith are very willing to grant that Christianity is a matter of " experience." If " the Christian experience " were a blank state of feeling without intellectual content, it would be ineffable and incommunicable ; it could not be the basis of a fellowship. It may be wise to refrain from defining doctrine too exactly and to lay little stress upon mere intellectual agreement, but obviously those who claim a common religion and are united in the fellowship of a Church must share a common faith. No common faith is possible without some common intellectual consent. Indeed, those who plead for an undogmatic Christianity are well agreed that God exists, and that He is revealed in Jesus Christ. Thus their real demand is for a minimum of dogma rather than no dogma at all. They would reject most of the old theologies and the phraseology of the creeds as lumber, but they cannot avoid some residue of unchanging intellectual agreement, if they claim that there is continuity in the Christian religion. Thus they restate but do little to illuminate our problem of defining the permanent and necessary and fundamental dogmas of the faith.

If a wholly undogmatic Christianity is a contradiction in terms (for the very name "Christianity" connotes some permanent relation to "Christ"), of what nature is dogma, and what is its basis?

What is permanent?

We may start from certain alleged dogmas of the faith. Christ "was crucified under Pontius Pilate" – is that dogma or only a fact of history? Christ "died for our sins" – does that belong to the permanent necessary dogmatic teaching of the Church or to the realm of theological interpretation which must change from age to age? Christ "descended into hell" – is that dogma or poetry or myth or history? Christ unites in His Person two natures, the divine and the human, which are conjoined inseparably and without confusion – is this necessary and permanent dogma or transient theological speculation? Upon what principle shall we determine what is permanent, and in what terms can we express it?

As regards the principle there are two answers, for the current practice whereby each man decides for himself what he regards as credible and necessary is not an answer, since it is no principle but that freedom which is perfect bondage. The Roman Church proffers one principle, historic Protestantism the other.

The Roman answer

The Roman Church claims an almost absolute finality for the statements of the creeds and for the dogmas which have been authoritatively defined, and this claim seems to cover the words as well as the substance of the formulæ. Dr. Karl Adam, who admits that the dogmas of the Church represent the Absolute but are not themselves the Absolute, is bound, as a Roman Catholic, to maintain that the creeds and authoritative definitions of the Church are binding upon the faithful in the terms in which they are officially set forth. This position rests upon the logically prior doctrine that the Church is so guided by the Holy Spirit that, when it speaks authoritatively, it cannot err, and upon the assumption that "the Church" in this context means the Roman communion.

This is one of those ultimates about which it is difficult to argue. But we may at least indicate some of the difficulties in the position. It is much easier to contend that there is a permanent validity in the creeds of the undivided Church than to make this claim for a series of further particular definitions set forth by a section of the Church which is out of communion with the rest. Such a proceeding seems purely arbitrary – in other words, it seems to rest upon some private illumination concerning which, since it has no rational basis, it is impossible to argue. There is the further objection that insistence is laid rather upon words than meanings; the words are sacrosanct; their interpretation is relatively free; but it would be more reasonable to suppose that words should be changing and meanings permanent, since we assume the changing element to lie not in the truth which is eternal, but in the variant fashions of speech and category.

Moreover, we are given no philosophical first principle to unify the very various pronouncements of dogma. The teaching of the Church, we are told, rests upon Scripture and tradition. But this is unsatisfactory, because Scripture is to be interpreted in the light of tradition, and this tradition is nowhere defined except in its announcements. Thus, for instance, such doctrines as of Transubstantiation, of the Immaculate Conception, of the Papal Infallibility, are deemed to have lain dormant or implicit or inchoate in the subconscious mind of the Church during a thousand years and more, when accepted saints and doctors might be wholly ignorant of them, or even violently repudiate them, until at last, by some supernatural gestation, they become the authoritative doctrine of a section of the Church in the form promulgated by authority. This is a position very hard to maintain once it has been clearly stated.

An Anglican answer

Many Anglicans have a theory which as a modification of this has much more to commend it. They accept as authoritative and, therefore, in some sense as final doctrine all that was accepted and promulgated by the undivided Church prior to the schism between East and West. Doctrine, they would say, rests upon Holy Scripture; this faith derived from Scripture is defined for all time in the acknowledged creeds and confessions of the undivided Church.

The Protestant principle of the Word

With much in this contention we may well agree. The creeds, in particular, define the central points of the Christian faith as the first Fathers understood it. It is idle for us to say, "the creeds express what the early Fathers supposed to be the substance of the Christian faith, but they were mistaken, and we know better"; for, though the creeds in their present form are relatively late, they have a known and traceable history back to the pages of the New Testament itself. If we wish to question the substance of any part of their profession, or indicate the impermanence of its form, it must be in consequence of some clear principle implied in their faith itself. In any event, we have already seen that, however unexceptionable this position be in theory, it is inadequate to answer our very proper question, What precisely are we to understand by the essence of the faith which the creeds set forth in the language of an earlier day?

In fact, we are either shut up to the letter which killeth or compelled to fall back on the Protestant principle which is covered by the phrase, "the Word of God." Thus, according to this second principle, Scripture, creed, and theology have sovereign authority only as they express and convey the Word. We must consider, therefore, this conception of the Word.

The phrase, "the Word of God," may be used in various senses. It is applied to Christ as the second Person of the Trinity; it is applied to the Bible as containing and conveying the Gospel; but in the sense in which according to historic Protestant doctrine the Word is said to be the foundation of the Church it means the Gospel. The creeds have validity and theological systems their excellence solely in the degree in which they are true expressions of the Gospel. If, therefore, we can define the Gospel, we have found the substance in distinction from the form, the permanent in distinction from the changing. It would be a glaring paradox if the Christian Church could not define its own Gospel; yet at first sight we have merely restated without illuminating our original problem by asking for a definition of "the Gospel" rather than of the substance of the creeds.

II

We must revert to the idea of revelation. The Christians claim that in Jesus Christ God has revealed not merely truths about Himself, but His very Self. When at Emmaus, in the breaking of bread, the Lord was recognized, the disciples were not in the first instance convinced of certain propositions concerning Him, though these might follow upon reflection ; rather, their apprehension was simple : " It is He ! " A flash of recognition, though it involve an act of the intellect, is simple and immediate ; it may later be elaborated into a proposition or series of propositions, but at the moment it is single, instantaneous, whole. St. Paul became a Christian through his experience on the Damascus road ; it might take him months or years or a lifetime to work out all that was implied in his sudden apprehension, but all was implicit in the moment of blinding vision. Similarly we may rightly define that ultimate experience which constitutes a man a Christian, or that ultimate affirmation which we call faith (for faith and experience are two sides of one event), as the apprehension of the living God in Jesus Christ. Such an experience or such faith is like a blinding flash. We must not assert that it is in the sphere of feeling as opposed to intellectual activity, for there is no feeling apart from thought, but clearly it is an apprehension which is not yet elaborated into the form of propositions. *Necessitas rationis est ex defectu intellectus ; certitudo rationis est ex intellectu.*

Revelation is simple

Further, as St. Thomas has amply shown, the Being of God is simple – that is, we cannot conceive Him as having parts in such a way that a man apprehending God should not apprehend the whole of Him so far as it is given to man to apprehend God at all. God's Word is one Word ;

But only expressible as a manifold

it is His Plan and Act in our salvation ; it may only be expressed by us in a series of propositions, but in itself it must be simple and undivided. God's Word can only be formulated by us in a series of words, and this series of words, as will be seen, must be in the form of narrative – "the old, old story."

We may perhaps illustrate the distinctive or creative Christian religious experience (which corresponds to the Christian revelation) by the poet's inspiration. His moment of inspiration is a rapture, a blinding flash, a moment of acutest receptivity when reflection and discursive thought are in abeyance, and he sees or hears or feels – or, better, understands – with an overwhelming intensity. Whether the rapture be brief or protracted, it is one moment, a whole, an undivided unity. It is followed by the labours of composition, sometimes slow and often careful, by which the poet attempts to find words for the adequate expression of his apprehension. The process is described in Shelley's essay on poetry. Inevitably there is loss. Though the poet be a master of his craft, and though his memory of the moment of high inspiration remain vivid, that which he can express must always fall somehow short of that which he has seen and felt.

It is not to be maintained that all poetical inspiration and composition conform to this pattern, but the illustration will serve its purpose and be generally intelligible, for most men know what it is to apprehend something with great vividness and then to be baffled in the verbal expression of the apprehension. The distinctive, fundamental Christian religious experience or revelation, it is here suggested, is parallel. The apprehension of God in Christ – be it in the breaking of the bread or on the road to Damascus, or on any and every other occasion, is a blinding flash ; it is the realization, " It is He ! " ; it is the apprehension, not of truths about God, but of God Himself ; it is His single Word, not yet broken up into sentences and propositions. It is not wholly ineffable, but there is always loss between the apprehension itself and its expression.

The Word and the creed

Such is the relation between the Word or revelation and the creed. The creed may express the necessary implications of the Word, but is never the mere transcript of the Word. It represents the Absolute, but is not the Absolute itself. We should abandon, then, the hope to find any formula, any verbal expression which shall be completely adequate and final. But if the Word or Gospel or revelation cannot be perfectly and finally expressed in human language, it does not follow that it cannot be expressed at all. It has already found innumerable expressions in creed and sermon, in hymn and prayer. There need be no reasonable doubt as to its substance.

The Word unchanging, theologies various

Thus in the New Testament the theology of St. Paul is not that of St. John, nor St. John's that of the author to the Hebrews, but there is no doubt that they shared a common faith, a common vision. It might be possible to find certain terms such as " Word " or " Messiah " which they would confess in common ; but their fundamental agreement does not in any way depend upon their using particular phrases in an identical sense. It is a unity that is apprehended by a sensitive judgment like that whereby one feels that three different instruments are in tune, or that a chord is accurately played. Christians agree that in the Epistles of St. Paul, in the Gospel and Epistles of St. John, in the Epistle to the Hebrews, the Gospel, the Word of God, is manifestly declared.

The task of disentangling the permanent substance

from the merely contemporary form is difficult but not impossible. It presupposes, however, a deep sympathy and understanding in the interpreter ; it can only be done with any precision within the Church. To the critic from without, the unsystematic theology of the apostle Paul, his profusion of metaphors, his multiplicity of categories are merely perplexing. But the Christian believer, to whom God has spoken in the glowing words of the apostle, who finds in the Epistles an expression of his own faith, has within himself the clue to the unity and intelligibility of the Pauline writings. No man, let us admit, has entered fully into the mind of St. Paul, for each man's mind is ultimately his own. But all the saints whose hearts have echoed to the apostle's words have understood, in greater or less degree, his meaning, and have consented to it. These same people have likewise entered into the Johannine writings and the Epistle to the Hebrews, and there, too, have found the same faith differently expressed.

Translation is difficult ; it can never be perfect, but it is not impossible. St. Paul represented Christ as the Second Adam ; to St. John He is the Logos ; in the epistle to the Hebrews He is shown as "an high priest for ever after the order of Melchizedek." These phrases are intelligible enough to scholars ; and no one doubts that for the ordinary person they need translation or gloss before they can be fully understood. The theology of the New Testament is altogether in this manifold and unsystematic form. The creeds are a crystallization and precise definition of the fundamental facts of the apostolic faith.

The criticism of the creeds

The criticism of the creeds is as necessary as of the apostolic writings. Anyone who accepts the religion of the New Testament finds in the creeds an expression of his faith, but not necessarily a perfect expression. Indeed, both the Apostles' Creed and the so-called " Nicene " Creed cannot be perfect because they are different. Why, for instance, does the Nicene Creed omit the words, " He descended into hell " ? Is it because this clause came to be regarded as untrue or unnecessary, and, if so, why? Or why does the Nicene Creed add " according to the Scriptures " to the statement that He rose on the third day? Is this addition necessary? Does it alter or define the sense? Or, once more, the Apostles' Creed says, " conceived by the Holy Ghost, born of the Virgin Mary " ; the Nicene says, " incarnate of the Holy Ghost by the Virgin Mary." Are these two assertions equivalent or different? If they are equivalent, the principle is established that the same truth may be asserted in different ways. If they are different, we have to ask why each creed omits something which to the other is essential. In their own way, though in a form less complicated than the canonical epistles, the creeds raise questions which only criticism can meet; and how can criticism be fruitful except on the assumption that the critic antecedently knows the faith which the creeds express and define?

If we trace the history of the creeds themselves, or contrast them with the great systems of theology and the more elaborate confessions which succeeded them, we note an ever-increasing complexity. Have we in these later statements genuine additions to the substance of the creeds, or merely the fuller indication of what is already implicit in them? And can we, taking the reverse journey, find some simpler statement of the Gospel of which the creeds are the more careful and precise definition? Can the Gospel be reduced to one idea from which all the more formal statements are derived?

III

The Gospel

We may offer two definitions of the Gospel in the words of Scripture: "God was in Christ reconciling the world unto Himself"; and, "God so loved the world, that He gave His only begotten Son, that whosoever believeth on Him should not perish, but have everlasting life." Both these statements, in different ways, are open to misconstruction, and therefore need further definition; and both have illimitable implications for thought and conduct. But each is a true statement of the Gospel. We can say with confidence that any theological proposition inconsistent with these definitions is to be condemned; but may we say that the whole Christian faith is implicit in these texts?

These two passages have been taken, not because none others are available, but because there will be no dispute among Christians that they represent the Gospel. They are simple in that peasants and rude men can understand their meaning; yet they involve for their intellectual elucidation the definition of "God," "Christ," "reconcile," "world," "love," "only begotten Son," "perish," "everlasting life." They imply the faith of the creeds, but they have the advantage or disadvantage that they are less precise and at the same time more simple than the creeds. How can this be?

Religion and theology

There must be some middle terms between the simplicity and indivisibility of that "blinding flash" which is the apprehension of God in Christ on the one hand, and the more or less abstract and metaphysical propositions of theology on the other. This is popularly recognized in the distinction between religion and theology. Thus many would regard the words "God sent His only begotten

Son " as an almost entirely religious statement, while the famous Chalcedonian definition of the Two Natures in Christ they would regard as pure theology – that is, human reflection in distinction from divine revelation. Many would regard the formula of the Nicene Creed – " God of God, Light of Light, very God of very God, being of one substance with the Father " – as an intermediate statement, partly religious, partly theological. That there is a distinction between a religious expression and a theological expression of the faith will be generally agreed. But how is the distinction in practice to be made? For instance, is the proposition, " God is Love," purely religious or also theological? If we could distinguish the utterances of religion from those of theology, we might find that we had distinguished substance from form, the permanent from the transient in the faith; for we should say that the religious statements are permanently valid, while the theological statements are of temporary significance.

Theology and dogma

The popular distinction between religion and theology is not happy, and is unlikely to commend itself to theologians. But I venture to put forward and defend a distinction between theology on the one hand and dogma on the other, and to suggest that dogma, in the sense to be explained, represents the permanent element in the Christian faith, and theology the transient. " There is," says Forsyth, " the theology which is a part of the Word, and the theology which is a product of it. There is a theology which is sacramental and is the body of Christ, so to say; and there is a theology which is but scientific and descriptive and memorial. There is a theology which quickens, and one which elucidates. There is a theology which is valuable because it is evangelical, and one which is valuable because it is scholastic." It is precisely this distinction which I would define, reserving the term "dogma" for "the theology which is part of the Word."

Dogma correlative to the Gospel

In connection with the idea of revelation, I said that the Christian apprehends God not only in what He *is*, but in what He *does*, and that the Christian revelation can only be expressed by active verbs, such as: God *sent* His Son; He *came* in Christ; He *reconciled*; He *took* our nature. The fundamental and distinctive dogmas of the Christian faith are not in terms of abstract truths about God, but in terms of "the mighty acts of God." The Christian sees "the mighty acts of God" in the coming, the death, and Resurrection of our Lord; further back he sees two all-comprehensive acts of God – the Creation and the Redemption; or, at last, one single mighty act of God, one divine dialectic, whereby the universe issues from God and returns to God. At every point the divine initiative, the divine energy, is dominant. The ultimate distinction between Natural Religion and the Christian faith lies in this – that Natural Religion apprehends God and divine truth through a contemplation of Nature and of history, whereas the Christian faith apprehends Nature and history in terms of the Incarnation; for Natural Religion truth is abstract and general, for Christian faith it is particular and concrete; Natural Religion (stimulated by Christian faith) declares in general terms that God is Love; the Christian faith asserts that God so loved that He sent His Son. This is another way of saying that Christianity is an historic religion, by which is here meant, not that it had for its Founder a particular historic Figure, but that it is indissolubly bound up with history.

Apart from its particular roots in history, Christianity would be a theosophy or philosophy of religion; it is its relation to history that constitutes it a Gospel. In connection with revelation it was indicated that integral to the Christian faith is the conviction that in Jesus Christ we find not a man who mirrors the character of God, but very God come to seek and save the lost. He spoke by the Prophets, but in the last days He sent His Son. The coming of the Son was not the raising up of a man to some perfection of prophecy, but the divine Condescension of God Himself.

The Gospel a story

Our mortal eyes are not able to see the pure white light ; we can only apprehend it in the many colours of the spectrum. We can, however, speak of the light which we cannot see. Not dissimilarly we can only express the divine action in a series of propositions concerning the birth, the death, the Resurrection and Ascension of the Lord ; we apprehend under the form of a time-series that which we can speak of as one single divine act in our redemption. We are apt to discuss and criticize the creeds as if they were a concatenation of separate propositions ; this they may be in form, but in substance they are asserting one fact and not many.

We have already noted the philosophical difficulties in the way of ascribing action to the changeless God. The Incarnation, which is the core of the Christian faith, is not, and cannot be, a strictly philosophical conception ; the Christian acknowledges that it is inscrutable mystery ; the critic properly asserts that in form it is not philosophical, but mythological.

The Christian Gospel implies many abstract or general truths, but it is not itself a series of such truths ; it is a *mythos*, a story, that God sent His Son. When we work out the implications of the story, we theologize ; but the unchangeable kernel of the Christian faith is not doctrine but story.

It is a thing most wonderful,
Almost too wonderful to be,
That God's own Son should come from heaven,
And die to save a child like me.

This is the story in a form so simple that children can grasp it ; this is the Gospel the implications of which must be worked out by theologians ; this is the fundamental dogma which involves many subsidiary or implicit dogmas, and is itself an ultimate of faith.

This contention must be elaborated and applied in later chapters. For the moment let it be understood to mean that dogma, in distinction from theology, is in story form wherein God is the agent, and the story declares His mighty acts.

The Condescension of God

Further, if the mythological – that is, the narrative – form is necessary to dogma, the problem of language is greatly simplified. From the nature of the case there can be no exactitude and adequacy ; at the same time there is no lack of definition. The propositions, " God was in Christ reconciling the world unto Himself," and, " God so loved the world that He gave His Son," are very different in form, but they point to the same apprehension and are identical in meaning. The same truth might be expressed in an indefinite number of forms, but, since each must declare the divine initiative and action, all must be mythological in form, and any statement will be true and equivalent which sets forth the inconceivable Condescension of God to the low estate of man. In this sense we may understand and approve the popular observation that the Divinity of Christ is the one dogma of Christianity.

The Word of God, then, is the Gospel, and the Gospel is

in form a story; for there is no possible formulation of it which does not imply the use of active verbs, such as God sent or took or came. In other words, the central and pivotal dogma of the faith is the Incarnation taken not as a metaphor (as, for instance, every good man or beautiful object may in some metaphorical sense be taken to be an incarnation of a divine idea), but in its proper sense of an inconceivable act of mercy on the part of Almighty God in human history.

We turn, then, to the application of this concept of dogma to the problems of theology and of the creed.

CHAPTER IV

NATURAL RELIGION: THE BIBLE

I

IN our search for the permanent substance of the Christian faith in distinction from its changing form we were led to a consideration of the specific character of the Christian revelation as Christians declare it. This we found to lie in the claim that in the Christian revelation it is God Himself who is revealed rather than truths about Him; or, in other words, the Christian claims to apprehend God not merely in His transcendent Being, but in His Action; He is revealed as the seeking and finding God, the reconciling God. Hence it was suggested that the distinctive Christian dogmas are expressed in terms of action – that is, in the form of a story which narrates "the mighty acts of God." This story may be summed up in the word "incarnation."

The Incarnation

But what precisely is meant by "incarnation" here? The term may be paraphrased in an indefinite number of ways. We may speak of the "divinity" of Jesus Christ, or may say that God came in Christ, or reconciled, or sent His Son, or took our nature. All of these phrases refer to the same apprehension or intuition; not one of them but is open to objection, since the terms, it may be said, are vague or mythological. But, while these phrases of necessity lack logical precision and adequacy, it is not at all obscure that they all seek to express some divine initiative and condescension, ἄφατος συγκατάβασις, apprehended in the historic Figure of Jesus Christ. The idea may be further defined by contrast or negation. Thus it is not meant that, God being in heaven, Christ reflects His glory as a lake reflects the moon; for, were that all that Christians would assert, they would have no ground for asserting a revelation other in kind than that of Natural Religion wherein God is apprehended through Nature, through beauty, and through human goodness. Again, it is not meant that Jesus Christ lived and worked *as if* God Himself were amongst men; for in that case the godlike One would be clearly distinguished from God Himself. Or, again, keeping to the language of the Gospels, we might say that the Christian revelation is no mere doctrine about God, but the apprehension that the Kingdom of God is come upon us. No phraseology is wholly satisfactory, but there is no doubt as to the nature of that apprehension to which all these phrases point.

Apprehended by faith

We may say that this divine condescension is apprehended by faith, if we mean by this that it is grasped by an intuition, not as the conclusion of a train of argument. But faith here must not be taken to connote uncertainty. We may consider the distinction drawn by St. Thomas between *intellectus* and *ratio*. The former points to a real grasping or penetration of truth by the mind, the latter to a search for truth by the way of discursive reflection that moves from point to point towards a conclusion. *Ratio*, or argumentation, is the sphere of theology; dogma is attained by a direct act of the understanding; it is akin to perception. But, even so, our apprehension is limited by the weakness of our mental powers. All understanding is *secundum modum intelligentis*, relative to the mental instrument. Hence this apprehension of truth can only be grasped by us in terms of mythology and symbolism.

The Gospel concrete

The Gospel is a story that "God so loved the world that He gave" His Son. This is not reducible to any abstract proposition. It is consistent with, and may involve, the truth that "God is Love"; but from the general principle of God's love we cannot deduce the concrete fact that God *so* loved that He gave. An unbeliever might consent to St. Thomas's proof that God is love and remain an unbeliever still. When, therefore, we relate dogma to "the mighty acts of God," we are thereby asserting that the language of dogma is mythological, or that dogma is only expressible through active verbs and in the form of narrative. From this, however, it does not follow that dogma is the work of phantasy in distinction from the strict thought of theology. On the contrary, it involves the highest act of the intellect, *simplex apprehensio*, and, further, it is couched in the necessary language of all religion that apprehends the living God as distinct from the changeless Being of philosophy and pagan mysticism.

We speak of the Incarnation when we think of the divine action, of the Redemption when we think of its effect. This Incarnation or Redemption is one single "mighty act" of God; but it is related to time, and can by us, therefore, only be set forth in terms of a story.

Articles of faith

This story has certain necessary parts, such as the birth, the death, the Resurrection of the Lord. There are, therefore, certain propositions necessary to the story; these may be called subsidiary dogmas or articles of faith. They are not yet theology, but its raw material. They represent the necessary implications or moments in the central apprehension, and they cannot be expressed with greater precision than that from which they are derived. Thus, for instance, that " Christ died for our sins " is an integral part of the story. As such, it is part of the subject-matter of theology which must relate the Atonement to the rest of thought concerning God, man, and the world. But, once again, we are not committed to a particular form of words. We may speak of " the Lamb of God," or " the cup of the New Covenant in my blood," without any alteration of the thought. The dogma is such because it is a necessary part of the story, not because it must be expressed in any particular form of words. It is possible and legitimate to question any form of words as inadequate to the thought, but the insertion of a direct negative into any such phrase (as, " Christ did not die, for our sins," or, " He is not the Lamb of God," or, " There is no new covenant in His blood ") is the denial of a necessary dogma and therein a repudiation of the faith.

We have now to relate dogma thus understood to philosophy or Natural Theology, to the Bible, to experience, and to authority.

II

Faith presupposes natural knowledge

St. Thomas says that many truths are known by revelation which also may be proved by the natural light of reason. If it were not so, he says, the knowledge of these truths would be hidden from all but those few who could follow the arguments. There is, and can be, no contradiction between Natural Religion and the Christian revelation. *Fides praesupponit cognitionem naturalem.* There is but one God who has revealed Himself in many ways and in many parts. We must, of course, recognize that all reception of truth is *secundum modum intelligentis*, or, in other words, that there is inevitably some distortion of truth in the human medium of prophet or poet; but no Christian should wish to deny the large measure of agreement which there may be between him and the man who, so far as the distinctively Christian revelation is concerned, is an unbeliever.

The distinctive element in the Christian revelation is in principle covered by the phrase "the Incarnation." Not only are several dogmas or articles of faith involved, as will be seen, in this fundamental concept, but much is presupposed in it. Thus the idea of the Incarnation presupposes the existence of God. Therefore the existence of God, as necessarily implied or given in the Christian revelation, is a dogma of the Christian faith. But the existence of God is recognized by mankind generally, and can be proved to be a necessary postulate of thought. Here, then, is a proposition which is at the same time a dogma of the faith and accepted doctrine outside the faith and a matter of logical demonstration. The Christian revelation is not an intuition that descends from heaven unrelated to the normal and necessary thought of rational beings. We may say, if we will, that the apprehension of God in Christ illuminates and transfigures all knowledge that was ours before, as the sun issuing from behind the clouds brings new colour and radiance to all the world; but there is much of the content of the Christian faith which, except in its colour and quality as part of a larger whole, is not distinctively Christian at all.

The Christian, as has been said, recognizes in sum two "mighty acts" of God – Creation and Redemption; for Redemption may be taken to cover all that leads up to the consummation of the Incarnation and all that follows from it, while Creation may be taken to cover not only the coming into being of the world, but its continuance in being.

Creation

Is the Creation, then, a Christian dogma? Creation, like Incarnation, is a term to cover a mystery. It is a mythological term rather than a philosophical. No one can ascribe to it a precise and intelligible meaning. But the thought which it expresses is both clear and necessary. Neither man himself nor this world nor anything in it is self-explanatory. Everything in the world is manifestly dependent on something else, relative to something else, and changing. The dependent, the relative, the changing presuppose the independent, the absolute, the changeless. God, therefore, the eternal, immutable, and self-sufficient must be postulated as the Ground of the world we know. This argument, here briefly summarized, is at once the proof of the existence of God and the indication of what the word " creation " means. When we say that God created the world out of nothing, we are not asserting a process which we comprehend or can imagine, but declaring that God is the Source and Ground of all that is. Here, again, we have a proposition that may be derived from philosophical reflection, that having been reached along various lines by poets and prophets has been taken up into Natural Religion, and that is involved in the Christian revelation. Doubtless, when the idea of Creation is combined with that of Redemption, much is added to the concept of Creation; but taken by itself Creation is both a dogma of the faith and a postulate of thought. The " humble believer " accepts the dogma that in the beginning God created the world, because, as will appear more clearly in our discussion of the Holy Trinity, it is involved in the fundamental Christian revelation of God in Christ, but the learned man or poet may hold the same view on different grounds.

Redemption

But is the Redemption a truth of the same kind? It may, perhaps, be realized by all sensitive minds that there is a sore wound at the heart of humanity, and that, if man is to be lifted out of himself and enabled to realize his spiritual destiny, there is need of grace, of some divine help and inspiration; and it may be very generally recognized, both within and without Christianity, that God has revealed something of Himself to man, and that either through the operations of Providence or in answer to prayer there is a divine help available.

A modern "restatement"

Those who go as far as this would freely admit that through Jesus Christ and the Christian religion pre-eminently this grace and help and inspiration have come to men. Among all the world's teachers none has brought such wisdom, such comfort, such benediction as Jesus Christ; among all the world's religions none has brought such peace and joy and victory as Christianity. These, it is said, are empirical facts; they are quite independent of the great doctrinal and dogmatic pronouncements of the Church; all this dogmatic superstructure is really an encumbrance to religion, an obfuscation of the simple truth. This conviction that in Jesus Christ we see the supreme religious teacher of human history, and that in the acceptance of His teaching lies the way of happiness and victory, is, it is said, the heart and substance of the Christian faith. All the rest is the mystification of the dogmatist or the commentary of pedants. When, therefore, we read that "God so loved the world, that He gave His only begotten Son, that whosoever believeth in Him should not perish but have everlasting life," we are to understand that God sent Christ as He sent Moses or

Socrates or Beethoven, that Jesus Christ, because of His filial attitude to God, is properly called in some special sense His Son, and that in following the teaching of Jesus Christ we have fellowship with God and eternal life.

This is, I think, the actual creed of many who " profess and call themselves " Christians. It is a religious position, which, as the fine flowering of Natural Religion, must win respect. I for my part confess that this is all so reasonable, so credible, so close to spiritual realities that it is to this position that in my moments of doubt I inevitably revert. This may prove in the end to be the ultimate truth and substance of Christianity, and, indeed, it may be set forth in a form hard to be distinguished from the Christian faith; but essentially it is not the Christian faith and is scarcely a pale reflection of it. I write with feeling here. I did not invent the Christian faith; I learnt it through the Bible and the Church. As a scholar I can define it objectively from the Bible and the Church's creeds and confessions, whether I believe it or not. My moods vary, my faith flickers; at best I cry, " Lord, I believe; help Thou mine unbelief." But in all moods I see clearly the difference between the historic faith of the Church and this modern parody of it which is but the common sense of all religious men.

The religious position here criticized may be summed up, as it often is summed up by its sponsors, not unfairly in the statement that the Christian religion is faith in the Fatherhood of God and the brotherhood of man, in the acceptance and practice of which creed we are encouraged and helped by the historic Figure of Jesus Christ. This is a beautiful religious faith, but demonstrably it is inadequate to such phrases as: " God so loved the world, that He gave His only-begotten Son"; "This cup is the new testament in My blood"; "conceived by the Holy Ghost, born of the Virgin Mary, suffered under Pontius Pilate, was crucified, dead, and buried, He descended into hell; the third day He rose again from the dead, He ascended into heaven, and sitteth on the right hand of God the Father Almighty"; "very God and very man." This is little more than a haphazard collocation from an indefinite number of possible and central declarations of the Christian faith. The view that I am criticizing is, for the most part, consistent with the faith, but quite certainly it does not express it; for, to revert to phraseology used above, it misses out the active verbs, or, in other words, it is precisely the distinctive element in the Christian revelation which it omits. It is a religious philosophy; it is not a story. It explains away the seriousness of the Incarnation as that event is understood in the Scriptures and by the Fathers of the Church, primitive, mediæval, and reformed. We could quote from St. Anselm, "*nondum considerasti quanti ponderis sit peccatum,*" and add to it *nondum considerasti quantae humilitatis sit Incarnatio*; you have as yet considered neither the gravity of sin nor the condescension of the Incarnation.

The Christian revelation transcends Natural Theology

We may conclude, then, that while the Christian revelation gathers up all the truth known of God through natural reason and Natural Religion, and while reason and natural piety may lead to the conclusion both that man needs redemption and that divine help is actually vouchsafed to him, yet the conviction that at a certain point in history God laid bare His mighty arm and in some sense walked Himself incarnate amongst men is not, as it cannot be, the conclusion either of speculative thought or of Natural Theology.

If it be replied that the ultimate standard and norm of

the Christian faith must be, not the theories of New Testament writers and later theologians, however venerable they be, but the teaching of Christ Himself, the answer lies to hand that this rationalized version of the faith is not in any degree a transcript of the teaching of the Gospels; it is, rather, a religious moralism based upon the Sermon on the Mount which, in its turn, is not a summary of the Christian faith, but a collection of the sayings of our Lord put together for the instruction of Christians in their Christian duty. The teaching of our Lord is shown in His miracles and in His death as well as in His words; nor can we estimate aright His words, if we have to explain away, "the Son of Man," "the Kingdom is at hand," "the New Covenant in My blood." Christian dogma has no source but the Person of Christ Himself.

III

The Bible as standard and rule of faith

Christianity with Judaism, of which it is the child, sees a unique significance in certain events in history. Hence the Bible, which records and interprets these events, is deemed to be unique literature. It has been the common doctrine of Protestantism, at least till very recent times, that the Bible is the standard and rule of faith. Even to-day there are few who wholly repudiate the doctrine. But, as so often, our difficulty here is that old phrases may be used with entirely new meanings, whereas the purpose of this study is to defend the view that, while words and explanations may vary, meanings must remain the same.

What precisely is the relation of Scripture to the Christian revelation? I will first put forward a view which I conceive to be widely held, though rather in the form of an

A modern view

assumption than of a stated doctrine: "the Old Testament is not Christian Scripture at all, but Jewish Scripture; it contains many passages of permanent devotional value, and the books as a whole must be studied by Christian scholars because they afford the historical, religious, and notional background of the New Testament. The New Testament, on the other hand, is certainly Christian Scripture; by this is not meant that it is in any unique way inspired by God, but it gives us the record of the Founder of our religion and the story of the first beginnings of the Church. It is, therefore, of permanent significance for the devotional and religious life of Christians. It must not be treated superstitiously, however. We must be ready to recognize that many of the thought-forms in which the early Church expressed its faith have ceased to have meaning for us; further, while the narratives are in the main trustworthy, we must anticipate and allow for the growth of legendary elements, and even in the case of the Gospels, especially the Fourth Gospel, we must exercise our critical faculty upon what we read, and attempt as best we may to rediscover the historic Christ behind the records. The New Testament, then, will always have a unique place in the hearts of Christians, but essentially it is not different from any other kind of literature."

Quite obviously, where this view obtains, the Bible is not the Word of God in anything like the same sense as it was to our fathers, nor is it even the ultimate standard and rule of faith, for the ultimate standard is plainly our own judgment of what is historically probable.

Over against this stands the doctrine of those who are called Fundamentalists. In its extreme expression this has sometimes been put in the form that every sentence

The Fundamentalist view

of the Bible, every word, every letter, was written down at the dictation of the Holy Ghost. The truth of everything in the Bible, therefore, is guaranteed by God Himself. In this extreme form the doctrine of the inerrancy of Scripture is open to unanswerable criticism. In the first place, it is not useful to declare that God dictated every word, unless we are in a position to know precisely what were the original words which He dictated. Every scholar knows that there are many passages in the Hebrew Scriptures which, as they stand, do not make sense, and, amid the varieties of New Testament manuscripts, it is impossible in many cases to fix with certainty the words that originally were written. Furthermore, there are, and there always have been, many passages of Scripture which have to be explained away by allegorical or other imaginative devices if every sentence must be ascribed to the God whom we know in Jesus Christ. In fact, Fundamentalists have always had to bring some extraneous principle of interpretation to the Scriptures. For instance, they have interpreted the New Testament in the light of traditional Protestant doctrine, and the Old in the light of the New. A norm for judging and interpreting Scripture implies that Scripture itself is not the rule of faith. Very few of the " results of Biblical criticism " can be regarded as " assured," but there can be no going back upon criticism itself. We may not seek to stifle the questions raised in the mind of modern educated readers by the Bible itself, as to the origin and authorship of its books, their dates, the value of their historical information, and the particular points of view presented by the authors.

The traditional doctrine of Protestantism which dates from before the rise of modern scientific historical and

The Protestant view

literary criticism must be reconsidered and revised. Happily what has become the traditional doctrine in this matter is not the doctrine of the Reformers themselves. They made a distinction between the Bible as a series of sentences and books, on the one hand, and the Word of God on the other. The Bible is our standard and rule of faith because it declares the Word of God which is the Christian revelation.

Biblical criticism has made us more clearly aware of the large human element in the Bible. The record comes to us through fallible human beings and subject to the vicissitudes of human literary transmission. The Bible is not miracle, but the record of miracle – that is, of "the mighty acts of God."

The Old Testament as Christian Scripture

The Old Testament begins with the Creation of the world and the Fall of man. I have written already about the Creation, and must come later to the Fall. With the Fall comes the "promise touching the saving seed" – "it shall bruise thy head, and thou shalt bruise his heel." From that moment the Old Testament becomes the record of the divine Redemption. It tells of the choosing of a peculiar people, their deliverance, their teaching by the Prophets, their schooling through suffering, their vision and their hardening of heart. It makes clear that the coming of the Son of Man was not unprepared nor unrelated to the past, but the end of its travail and the fulfilment of its promise.

God, Who when Enoch on the earth was holy
Saved him from death, and Noë from the sea,
Planned Him a purpose that should ripen slowly,
Found in Chaldaea the elect Chaldee –

God, Who for sowing of the seed thereafter
Called him from Haran, summoned him from Ur,
Gave to his wife a weeping and a laughter,
Light to the nations, and a son to her –

God, Who, to glean the vineyard of His choosing,
Sent them evangelists till day was done,
Bore with the churls, their wrath and their refusing,
Gave at the last the glory of His Son.

The Old Testament is Christian Scripture not because of its purple passages nor because of any guaranteed inerrancy in its language, but because of its story. It tells not ordinary history, but, as the Germans say, *Heilsgeschichte*, the story of our salvation.

But, while the Old Testament declares for Christians part of the Christian revelation, and thus is sacred Scripture, it has a wholly human side: it may be studied like any other collection of ancient books. The history may be checked, the authors tested and questioned; their point of view may be indicated and criticized. Those narratives which in the Bible are represented as the works of God may be put in their secular setting and reinterpreted so that their divine significance is lost. To the ear of faith the Old Testament tells of the "mighty acts of God" in man's redemption; to the eye of the unbeliever the story of Israel is parallel to that of Moab, of Egypt, or of Assyria.

If a Christian of the early centuries were asked when the Church began to be, it is likely that he would not answer that the Church was born at Pentecost or Easter. He might reply that, as the Church is part of the eternal counsel of God, it was created before the sun and the stars; but, historically, he would date the Church from the Call of Abraham or the covenant with Noah. The Old Testament is Christian Scripture precisely because it is the record of that "mighty act of God" in our redemption which culminated in the Incarnation. It tells the first chapter of that *mythos*, that narrative, which is the Christian revelation.

The New Testament as Christian Scripture

Into the very difficult theological problems connected with the formation of the Canon we cannot enter here. It must suffice that the New Testament is Christian Scripture for the same reason that it records the Christian revelation. Two comments will be in place. First, we have seen that there can from the nature of the case be no precision of language in man's attempt to express the apprehension of the living God in the Person of Jesus Christ. In its simplest form the story is that "God so loved the world, that He gave His only begotten Son," but the same thing may be said in many ways and elucidated in many metaphors. We may speak of the Coming of the Son of Man, or of the Second Adam, or of the high priesthood after the order of Melchizedek, or of the Lamb of God, or of the Word made flesh. These phrases are, to use logical phraseology, identical in denotation, but not in connotation – that is to say, they all point to one identical Person or event, but each illustrates the subject from a different angle. The man who has grasped the central idea, who has apprehended the heart of the revelation, understands all these terms – or, at least, understands that at which they point; the man who has not grasped the central truth, that in Christ we apprehend the Presence of God Himself come for our redemption, can merely explain, and explain away, all these metaphors and images in terms of their human origin. There is one key to unlock all these terms. If we have faith we understand ; if we have not faith, we see only unsystematic theology and inapposite metaphors.

Second, the New Testament itself is not Holy Scripture except to faith. As Jesus Christ Himself appeared among men as one amongst many, and was taken by most of His contemporaries as Rabbi or Prophet or Pretender, according to their spiritual vision, and only to the few was manifest as the Son of God, so the New Testament may be read by modern students. Sometimes, as they read, the veil may be taken from their eyes, and here and there one and another will " behold His glory " and pierce through His incognito ; but apart from faith – that is, apart from an acceptance of the Christian revelation – the New Testament is simply a series of writings that must somehow be explained away.

The evangelists set before us the earthly story of the divine Son of God, the Word made flesh. The ordinary reader naturally approaches the Gospels with the assumption that they rest upon a misapprehension. To him, St. Mark's Gospel, which is often commended not only as the earliest, but the most human, must appear frankly incredible, for the whole narrative is marked throughout by the supernatural and miraculous. It is therefore the often unconscious presupposition of the reader that the narrative cannot, as it stands, be true ; he must therefore all the time be attempting to discount the narrative and to reach to the historic Figure who is buried beneath the accretions of legend and the theological assumptions of the writers.

Says the Russian novelist, Merezhkowsky : " Which is He, myth or history, shadow or substance ? . . . It would never enter anyone's head to ask whether Jesus had lived unless, before asking the question, the mind had been darkened by the wish that he had not lived. . . . The thief requires that there should be no light ; the world that there should be no Christ." The efforts made and remade to prove that Christ never existed are relatively crude, but there is, and will be, no end to the Lives, Studies, and learned monographs aimed to prove that He was not what the Gospels say He was. This should be no matter for surprise, partly because His coming, as depicted in Scripture, is the judgment and condemnation of the world, and partly because our reason staggers at the thought of Incarnation. *Credo quia impossibile*, says one great believer ; I believe because it is impossible – that is, I believe, for only faith could hold to that which so far transcends all common sense.

Historical criticism

Modern historical scientific criticism is making more and more difficult the purely humanistic interpretation of the Gospels, but the effort must be made, for there is no choice but humanism or the Gospel. "In 1932," says Merezhkowsky, "He is the Unknown, as much an enigma, 'a sign that shall be spoken against,' as He was in the year 32. The miracle of His being in history is a perpetual stumbling-block to mankind ; it is easier to repudiate history than to accept it with this miracle." Again : "To read 'the Life of Jesus' in the Gospel, it is not enough to know history ; one must see what preceded it, what has followed it – the beginning of the world and the end – one has to decide which is to predominate ; whether Jesus is above history, or whether history is above Him ; and which is the criterion : whether He is to be judged in the light of history, or whether history is to be judged in relation to Him. By the former method it is impossible to discover Him in history – that is possible only by the second method. Before perceiving Him in history we must perceive Him in ourselves." The New Testament plainly declares the Christian revelation; but, if that revelation be not accepted, some theory or device must be found to explain the New Testament away. Not a little modern criticism amounts to no more than this.

But this must not be taken to imply a going back upon New Testament criticism and a reversion to what is known as "Fundamentalism." Criticism is both unavoidable and salutary. But it will easily be seen that if Jesus Christ really was that which the New Testament and the Church have always declared that He was – the Son of God, the Word incarnate – then very much of what passes for criticism is beside the mark.

Therefore, it is because, and in so far as, the Scriptures of the Old and New Testaments declare the Word of God, which is the Gospel of the gracious acts of God in man's redemption, that the Scriptures are the standard and rule of faith for Christians. Thus the Bible is brought into the most intimate relation with revelation, while there is no need whatever to question the large human element in its formation. The Word is the Gospel which is the revelation; its record lies in Holy Scripture.

The impregnable Rock

Hence it is said that the Church rests upon the impregnable Rock of Scripture. But there are believers who very properly object that the Church was in existence before the New Testament was written, and that the New Testament issues from the faith and tradition of the Church. Therefore, it is argued, Scripture rests upon the Church, not the Church on Scripture. This is so; but the true Protestant principle was mis-stated. We should not claim that the Church rests upon the Bible, but that the Church is created by, lives by, and therefore rests upon the Word of God, the revelation, the Gospel, which is recorded once for all in Holy Scripture. The divine revelation is prior both to Church and Scripture. We must come, therefore, to a consideration of the relation between the revelation and personal religious experience.

Chapter V

EXPERIENCE: AUTHORITY

I

IT is obvious that revelation and religious experience are related, since, if there is revelation, there must be someone to whom the revelation is made; but in popular speech it is customary to distinguish, almost as contraries, dogma and experience. To which, then, does faith belong? One school says that faith is essentially a matter of personal religious experience; the other that faith is the acceptance of Christian dogma. Is faith, then, related more closely to emotion or to obedience?

Faith

"Faith" is a term that may be used in two senses: it may be *fides qua creditur* or *fides quae creditur* – that is, it may be that consent of the mind whereby we believe, or it may be the contents of the mind when we believe. These two senses are in no way contradictory. We cannot hold the Christian faith except through some act of submission to it, and, on the other hand, we cannot have faith without some intellectual content; if we believe, we must believe something. None the less, two schools of thought are far apart: there are Romanists who seem to make faith primarily an act of intellectual obedience; there are Protestants who seem to make it almost entirely a matter of emotion. The former relate faith closely with authority, the latter regard it as inseparable from personal and individual vision. There is a wide difference between those who say that their faith rests on authority, and those who say it rests upon " experience."

The authoritarian view

Let me put, first, the authoritarian view. The Christian faith, it is said, rests upon the testimony of the prophets and apostles. This testimony in its turn rests upon personal experience, upon fellowship with the incarnate Word and upon the Resurrection appearances. Ultimately therefore, dogma rests on experience, but not on our experience. The intellectual elaboration of the primitive deposit of faith is the business, not of the individual, but of the Church as a whole, and, in particular, of its theologians. The faith is an indivisible whole, but its necessary implications go far beyond the intellectual grasp of simple Christians who yet are indubitably Christians, being nourished by the Church's life, and accepting as the way to God that religious discipline and those means of grace which the Church provides, and therein implicitly accepting the supernatural truths upon which the Church and its institutions rest. But it is not for them to grasp the mystery of the Holy Trinity or to understand how Christ died for our sins. By an act of faith they accept the Church. Their personal experience is genuine and necessary, but doctrine they must take on authority – that, for most, can never in this world be a matter of personal experience.

The individualist view

The opposite view may thus be put : our faith is that which we ourselves believe ; it is an intimate, personal matter ; it is, ultimately, trust in a Person and not the acceptance of any doctrines whatsoever. We cannot accept any doctrines except in so far as they answer to something in our own experience ; whatever notions we may temporarily take on trust from other people do not belong to faith in any religious sense. We believe in

Christ; therefore we are Christians; we do not accept any doctrines which are not reflected in our personal experience.

Not contradictory

These two views are much nearer together than would at first sight appear. It seems that to say, "I believe in the Church, therefore I accept all the Church's teaching," is as far as possible removed from the position, "I believe in Christ, but I do not accept any doctrine that does not commend itself to my own judgment." But the starting-point of the two positions is substantially identical. The Romanist says, in effect, "I believe in the Church," where the Protestant says, "I believe in Christ," but what is the difference in substance? It would be equally true, in fact, to say that the Romanist believes initially in Christ, and the Protestant in the Church. For it is, in fact, impossible to trust the Church without trusting Christ or to trust Christ without trusting the Church.

Thus, the Romanist has found in the discipline, the rites, the worship of the Church some experience of God in Christ which answers to his spiritual need. For the discipline, the rites and worship of the Church have no possible meaning apart from God in Christ, nor can the Romanist believe the teaching of the Church except upon the basis of this acceptance of Christ. He accepts Christ in and through the Church; therefore he accepts that doctrine which men wiser than he aver to be involved in his experience.

The Protestant likewise finds Christ through the Church – not, perhaps, through the ceremonies and public worship of organized Christianity, but certainly through Christians who tell him about Christ; he accepts, in fact, the testimony of the prophets and apostles as this comes to him through the Christian fellowship. Since this faith in

Christ is so intimately personal and individual, he declares that nothing can belong to it which comes to him merely on authority without any inward testimony of the Holy Spirit in his own heart. While the Romanist accepts implicitly all that the Church teaches, the Protestant puts on one side all that is not real to him.

There is a genuine difference here, but it must not be put in the form that the Romanist believes the Church while the Protestant believes *in* Christ. For both believe in Christ, and both believe the Church. But the Romanist is prepared to accept on authority that which he cannot understand, and the Protestant is not.

Danger of authoritarianism

Both these views, if pressed to an extreme, lead to a position that cannot be commended. There can be no doubt that the Roman system has led to serious abuses. The Church has been content with the implicit faith of the laity, and, so far from making adequate efforts to instruct them in the faith, has too often been very content that they should remain in ignorance of much of it. Further, the requirement of passive obedience to dogma as officially defined has led to grievous conflicts in the hearts of many between their religious convictions and their intellectual integrity.

Danger of individualism

But the Protestant position, if pressed to an extreme, as it is by many to-day, is in a fair way to lead to the complete disintegration of Protestantism itself. "I believe in Christ," says one, "but as for the traditional doctrines of the Trinity, the Incarnation, the Atonement, they really mean nothing to me; I certainly could not say that I believe them. That which constitutes a Christian is faith in Christ. I have faith in Christ, therefore these doctrines are unnecessary encumbrances; they cannot belong to the essence of the Christian faith." In other words, the Christian faith may be defined by the limits of any individual experience. Few draw this conclusion explicitly, but it inevitably follows from the argument.

The position needs further analysis. We ask this type of Protestant: "When you say that you believe in Christ, what precisely do you mean?" We may receive any of three very different answers. First, he may say, "I believe in Christ because of a profound religious experience. I can no more describe this experience than I can describe the scent of new-mown hay; the experience is too intimately personal for any further definition." If we receive this answer, no further argument is possible. Such a position spells the end of the Church; for there cannot be a Church except upon the basis of a common faith, and a faith that cannot be defined except in a phrase that might mean almost anything is not, except by accident, a faith that can be shared in common.

The second answer may take many forms, but in substance it is this: "When I say that I believe in Christ, I mean that I do not accept the traditional theology of the Church, nor even the theology of the apostle Paul; I believe in the Christ of the first three Gospels." This much more common answer presupposes that the Christ of the Gospels is distinguishable from the Christ of traditional Christian faith. In other words, it really implies that faith in Christ as understood by the speaker is something other than faith in Christ as the Church understands it. If this means that the speaker is not satisfied with the adequacy or necessity of traditional theological formulæ, we may be content. But almost invariably the protest means that the Church has misrepresented the human Figure of the Gospels, and by its elaborate theology concerning Him whom it calls "very

God " as well as " very man " has contorted a simple message into an unintelligible dogma. Now, it can be demonstrated that what we conveniently and briefly call " the divinity of Christ," or the belief in Christ as the incarnate Son of God, is presupposed by all the evangelists ; and, when a man says that he rejects the theology of the Church, but accepts the Christ of the Gospels, he almost invariably means that he rejects the Christ of the Gospels and substitutes for Him some imaginary picture of a Christ who is supposed to lie behind the distortion of the Gospels. Thus we have a real, though often unconscious, denial of that which we have seen to be the distinctive element in the Christian revelation. For no man who has apprehended in Christ the very condescension and presence of God Himself would think of saying that he rejects the theology of the Church but accepts the first three Gospels. Thus the phrase " faith in Christ " may often imply the denial of what the Church means by the Christian faith. Protestantism, at the moment, is full of persons who in spirit, temper, and outlook are very Christian, but who have no grasp whatever upon the fundamentals of the faith, and who, if challenged, will reply that it is spirit and conduct that matter, not beliefs. It is not the purpose of this book to exalt beliefs above spirit and conduct, but it must be obvious that the Christian religion cannot endure apart from the Christian faith.

The third answer to our question may be : " I believe in Christ as I read of Him in the Gospels, but I am no theologian ; I am puzzled and perplexed by the doctrines that the Church expounds, and I am content simply to believe in Him." To this we should be able to reply : " To be a Christian believer it is not necessary to be a theologian; if you really believe in Christ as He is given to us in the Gospels, you implicitly believe the dogmas of the Church, as we could prove to you, had you the interest and ability to follow the argument." This, it will be noticed, is very near to the Roman answer, but there is this most important difference – that Protestantism starts from one single principle, the Word of God, the Gospel, and its whole theology should be logically deducible from that. The Roman Church does not attempt to show that every dogma proceeds necessarily from the revelation given once for all. For many propositions declared by the Roman Church to be *de fide* – that is, binding upon believers – no authority can be adduced beyond the contemporary authority of the institution that propounds them.

The authority of the Church

What, then, do we conclude, is the relation between dogma on the one side and personal experience on the other? Dogma we have defined as a statement or necessary implication of the central and ultimately all-inclusive or all-involving revelation which we call the Incarnation. It is eminently possible that a man should apprehend, or begin to apprehend, the Incarnation – that is, should begin to believe that Jesus Christ is the Son of God, without realizing many of the necessary implications of this faith; he may cry out with St. Thomas, "My Lord and my God!" and yet, presented with the Athanasian Creed or any other formal statement of doctrine, he may say, "That means nothing to me," or, "I cannot see that such a doctrine is involved in my simple faith." None the less the Church very properly says: "This doctrine is really involved in your faith; this is ground that has been traversed again and again by the pious and learned in the Church; our doctrine, we agree, is not an adequate or perfect statement of the mystery; but, if you had time to study that doctrine, and to ascertain what it really states, you would certainly find that your faith involves it; or, if you did not, you would see that you have not meant by the words, 'My Lord and my God,' what the Church means by them."

Therein is seen the true and proper authority of the Church. A man is scarcely in a position to reject or criticize as inadequate a dogma which he does not understand. Nothing more vividly displays the very perilous amateurishness into which much of Protestantism has fallen than the light-hearted way in which ministers and laymen will boast that they do not accept the doctrine of the Trinity or of the Person of Christ or some other central dogma, while they make it abundantly clear, in the very utterance of their incredulity, that they do not understand what they reject. The Roman Church is to be commended in so far as it requires a humbler and soberer attitude to the wisdom of the saints and Fathers.

Dogma and experience

Still we have not answered our question as to the relation of dogma to religious experience. A dogma or article of the faith, it has been here maintained, is an integral part of the story which is the Gospel. How can part of a story be a matter of our private experience? "Suffered under Pontius Pilate" is a necessary part of the story; that event may be part of our knowledge, but it can no more be part of our experience than is the Battle of Hastings. Again, "He died for our sins, and not for our sins only, but also for the sins of the whole world" – that is an integral part of the story. That He died for my sins might, perhaps, be a matter of my personal experience, but that He died for my neighbour's sins cannot belong to my experience, though it may be a matter of my personal conviction. Or, again, the Creation of the world can be neither my experience nor any man's. Therefore, unless we are using "experience" in some unusual sense, we cannot assert that all Christian dogma rests upon either my personal experience (which would in any case be a Titanic absurdity) or upon the experience of the Church or of the human race. The dogmas or articles of the faith are the propositions necessary to thought when we reflect upon the Christian revelation. There is, as will appear, a profound truth in the assertion that dogma must conform to Christian experience, but it is not the absurd statement or assumption that the feelings or emotions or guesses of the pious or enthusiastic are a standard of truth or of validity in Christian doctrine. It is one thing to relate all dogma to that experience of God in Christ which is the fundamental Christian revelation; it is another thing altogether to make the absence of subjective religious "experiences" the ground for the repudiation of Christian doctrines. Dogma belongs to the sphere of thought, not of emotion.

Yet the contention that dogma must be related to experience is, if soundly interpreted, both fruitful and illuminating. It corresponds with the contention of this whole book – that all Christian theology should spring from the Word of God, and that every dogma must be an expression of the Word.

The Christian faith is the expression of the Christian revelation. Revelation presupposes some person or persons to whom the revelation is made. It must be received by the whole self of the recipient, but the predominant organ of revelation is the mind. There is no thought without feeling; therefore the reception of revelation cannot be apart from feeling; but the psychological concomitants of revelation are of very tertiary importance. Because the term "experience" is popularly connected first of all with feelings, it is an unsatisfactory term; but, in so far as it indicates that revelation is received not without the will and the feelings, it is suitable. Certainly the revelation that came to prophets and apostles was their experience in this better sense. Certainly, also, no man will accept the testimony of the prophets and apostles unless his mind and heart have been quickened so that, at least in some dim way, the experience or revelation of the prophets and apostles has come to him also. In other words, only by faith can the Christian testimony be accepted, and faith is not the conclusion of a syllogism but the answer of the heart – that is, of the whole man – to a spiritual perception. Whether in Romanism or Protestantism faith must come first; it may be called faith in the Church or faith in Christ, but at bottom it is some ultimate apprehension of the personal action of God upon the soul through Christ. This apprehension may be clearer or dimmer, but it must be "through Christ" if it is to be a distinctively Christian faith.

God reveals Himself through Christ and in Christ to the believer; this is the fundamental Christian revelation or, subjectively put, experience. But the definition is still inadequate. Many who are not, and who make no claim to be, Christians, as, for instance, many Hindus, would confess that to them also God has spoken through Christ. Indeed, any theist who claims to find the revelation of God in moral as well as æsthetic beauty would agree that Jesus Christ is a revelation of God. Therefore there must be some distinctive Christian revelation of God in Christ whereby a man is constituted a Christian believer. When we consult the New Testament and the creeds and confessions of the Church, it is plain what is this distinctive element. It is the recognition of the Incarnation. It is this which distinguishes the Christian faith from all other philosophies and religions which in greater or less degree are tinged with Christianity. The Christian sees in Christ One who "though He was rich yet for our sakes became poor"; the Christian apprehends the Majesty of God "in the form of a servant." That is a religious apprehension, or, if the phrase be preferred, a religious experience, out of which arises the whole of Christian theology. Therefore all theology rests upon the religious experience of believers.

Here, then, we have in our hand a norm of the utmost importance for the testing of traditional theology. If a traditional doctrine be shown to be a misrepresentation of the story, the basic apprehension, the fundamental experience, it must inevitably stand condemned. An illustration will suffice: John Calvin, in attempting to think out the implications of the divine Providence and the gravity of sin, was led to the doctrine of the predestination of many souls to eternal reprobation. It is idle for us to say that we do not like the doctrine, or find nothing in our individual religious experience which corresponds to it, for that is to make our preferences or our limited and confused experience the test of truth. But if we can show that the image of the Shepherd leaving the ninety and nine to seek the lost sheep "till he find" is integral to the story which is the Gospel, then we must without hesitation reject any doctrine inconsistent with it. All Christian doctrine rests upon experience, but only because all rests on revelation.

The response to the Christian revelation is inevitably worship and love; these are moments in the religious life prior to formulated dogma or theology. "We love Him because He first loved us." Thus, again, theology rests upon experience, but it is safer and wiser to say that all theology rests upon that Word of God, that revelation, which awakens our adoring love.

II

The authority of the Word

Our discussions have already dealt by implication with a large part of the relations of dogma to authority. In accordance with strict Protestant theology it has been maintained that the ultimate authority in the Christian faith is the Word of God. The meaning of this phrase " the Word of God " should by now be plain. It is not identical with Scripture, but it is that Gospel of our redemption, presupposing our creation, to which the Scriptures bear witness. The Word of God is the Gospel, which, in its turn, is the proclamation of " the mighty acts of God." Thus the Gospel is necessarily in narrative form and concrete ; it is not a series of general ideas or truths about God's Nature and Being, but a glad tidings of what God has done – " He hath visited and hath redeemed His people."

Dogma stands in no contrast to reason. The truths of revelation, like any other truths, are apprehended by our intellect. Dogma asserts nothing in contradiction of that which may be known by the natural light of reason ; moreover, the intimation of what dogmas are inherent in the Christian revelation is itself a work of reason, not emotion. Much that is known by revelation is likewise to be known by reason. The Word of God itself is subject to reason in that it can only be apprehended by reason and considered by reason. But reason which is competent to deal with the facts presented to it is not creative of them.

As the scientist exercises his reason upon the data presented by his science, so the theologian exercises his reason upon the datum of revelation. But the revelation itself is something given by God and apprehended by faith, not achieved by abstract thinking. We might conceivably, by pure thought, attain to the conviction that God is Love, but reasoning of itself will no more give us the truth that "God so loved the world that He gave" His Son than it will give us Magna Carta or the Treaty of Versailles. In the Christian faith the datum, the given or revealed element, is the ultimate authority, and this is "the Word of God."

Again, the Bible derives its authority from the Word; it is a work of human activity, and shows many signs of its human origin; it carries within itself no guarantee of supernatural inerrancy; its authority is derived from the Word, which it declares and conveys. As the vehicle of the Word, but not otherwise, it is the standard and rule of faith.

But what is the authority of the Church in respect of dogma? The Church, again, is wholly subject to "the Word" of which it is both the witness and the product. Obviously the Church can have no authority over against the Word that created it. But what is the Church's authority in the definition of the faith?

Modernism

There is a school within modern Protestantism which says in effect: "We are Christians; but from the height of our modern point of view we can see that even from the first the Church has developed its thought along wrong lines. The apostle Paul led the way, when he substituted the gospel *about* Jesus for the Gospel *of* Jesus. The early Fathers made matters worse with their trifling and irrelevant distinctions. The false intellectualizing of the scholastics completed the utter misrepresentation of the original Gospel. The Reformers tried to simplify and to return to Christian sources, but they lacked the necessary Biblical science for their project ; thus, in fact, they took over the traditional debased form of Christianity in its essentials. When, therefore, we speak of a restatement of the Christian faith, we do not think of yet another version of the doctrine of the Trinity or of the Person of Christ or of the Atonement ; we mean a radical reconstruction of the whole notion of Christianity, for at last, thanks to our criticism, we are in a position to understand the Master." In other words : "We propose to set forth a faith radically different from that of historic Christianity, but to serve ourselves heir to the goodwill of the name."

It is not surprising that modernism has been defined as "the abandonment of the Christian faith coupled with an unwillingness to take the consequences." If these reformers propose to declare that the Word of God which the Church of Christ has always proclaimed is not the true Word, they can have no kind of title to the name of Christian. If, on the other hand, they declare that it is the same Word, they must produce some real equivalent of the faith they would improve. The crucial issue is the Incarnation, the faith that the Majesty of God took "the form of a servant." If they deny that, or explain it away, they have repudiated as a delusion the Christian revelation. If they affirm that, then, since reason and logic do not vary, they must ultimately come to something very like the old orthodox theology.

The Church on earth has a very human aspect : it is composed of sinful and weak and ignorant human beings, liable always to err and incapable of any perfection. Therefore, as has been sufficiently indicated, there can be no finality or ultimate adequacy about their definitions or their theories. If God has guided their thoughts, still it has been *secundum modum intelligentis*, subject to the limitations of their powers of reception. Yet, if we claim to know better what the Gospel is than did St. Paul and St. John and St. Ambrose and St. Augustine and St. Bernard and St. Francis and St. Thomas and Luther and Calvin and Hooker and Wesley and Spurgeon, and if we claim that the Christian faith is really something quite other than they supposed, it would be well for us to cultivate a sense of humour.

But I am dealing with extreme, if not uncommon, cases. There are many who are prepared to pay a passing tribute to the œcumenical creeds as documents of historic interest and importance, and to regard with a rather superior respect the theologies of their grandfathers, but are convinced that in the present day the Christian faith must be radically restated. It is idle, they say, to seek to refurbish the old theories and to try to put modern meanings into the old phrases.

With the claim that the Christian faith must be restated I for one am in profound agreement. It might even be urged by the indulgent that this book is an essay in that direction. But, if I may anticipate the argument of later chapters which will elucidate the point in particular, I would indicate here that the limitations of restatement are set by logic and not by prejudice, and that, however much the form of expression and elaboration may change, there is an enduring dogmatic element, constituting the substance of the Gospel, which is much more extensive than innovators at first suppose. The "story" and its implications do not change. If we desire to tell another story, or to substitute for the story a philosophy of religion, we have abandoned the Christian revelation. Our subsequent chapters on " The Content of Dogma " might as well be entitled " The Necessary Implications of Faith in the Incarnation."

The Church and the Word

The authority of the Church is clear. The Church is empowered and required to define and expound the Word which constitutes it. The Word cannot be other than the Church declares it to be. We may accept or reject the Church's Gospel, but we may not say that the Church's Gospel is not what the Church says it is. But the Church's definitions and expositions of the Word may be tested by the Word itself declared in Scripture. As the sheep know the voice of the shepherd, and to the voice of a stranger will they not hearken, so believers, who themselves have in some measure apprehended God in Christ, as Christians mean the phrase, and who have the Scriptures before them, are able both by the exercise of logic and by a certain sensitiveness of the spiritual ear to judge of the harmony or discord between the Word and any particular formulation or definition of it. We turn, therefore, to consider in greater detail the positive content and implications of " the Word."

Part II

THE CONTENT OF DOGMA

CHAPTER VI

THE HOLY TRINITY

Introductory

THE purpose of this chapter is to show that the assertion of the Trinity – that is, that the Deity is Three Persons in One God – is a dogma of the faith. Hence, if anyone should deny the Trinity knowing what his words meant, he would be repudiating the Christian revelation. I stress the phrase, " knowing what his words meant," for we need not take too tragically the cheerful denials which rest on ignorance.

To some the very attempt will seem a paradox or counsel of despair. They are prepared to admit that much in Christian theology is derived from, and implied in, the first three Gospels, but the doctrine of the Trinity they regard not as the supreme mystery of the faith, but as the supreme mystification of the theologians. They see in it the signal illustration of the substitution of metaphysics for religion; they cannot admit that faith in Christ requires of them the assertion of a doctrine so tortuous and so incomprehensible; they may even quote the observation that in the opinion of theologians the Athanasian Creed alone succeeds in accurately stating the doctrine, and this it achieves only in virtue of following every assertion by its formal contradiction.

There is force in this. The traditional doctrine of the Trinity is highly abstract, metaphysical, and paradoxical – so much so that it can only be understood by philosophers, and is rarely stated accurately even by theologians. None the less, it remains true that to cry out with an understanding heart, "Glory be to the Father and to the Son and to the Holy Ghost," is almost the beginning and the end of Christian prayer and worship.

I have ventured to distinguish revelation, dogma, and theology in this way: revelation is the act of God opening our eyes to behold His glory in the face of Jesus Christ; dogma corresponds to the affirmations which we are bound to make when we attempt to express the logical and spiritual implications of revelation; theology is the systematic attempt to relate dogma to the whole of knowledge, and to present it in the form of explanation or philosophical and articulated expression. Thus, to revert to an earlier illustration, revelation corresponds to the poet's moment of rapture, dogma to the poem (in this case, an epic poem), and theology to gloss, paraphrase, and exposition.

The distinction in theory is clear; in practice it cannot be absolute; for revelation in the very moment of its occurrence, however "blinding" it be, cannot be wholly devoid of intellectual content, and thus be wholly separated from dogma, while, on the other hand, dogma cannot be divided by a hard-and-fast line from theology. Thus, for instance, "God so loved the world that He gave His only begotten Son" is a statement (though not the only possible form of statement) of the act of God made known to us in revelation; it is concrete and in narrative form; it belongs to the sphere of dogma, not of theology; it is the subject matter of theology. But the proposition, "God is Love," is a general, abstract principle which may be derived from the dogma that God sent His Son. As belonging to systematic exposition it is a proposition in theology. On the other hand, if it is a necessary implication of the Christian revelation, though it be not actually a part of the Christian "story," it may be deemed, in a subsidiary sense, a dogma of the faith. Further, in the case of theology, which is concerned with the logical and systematic exposition of dogma, language must so far as possible be exact and reasoning rigorous. But in respect of dogma, which reflects "the mighty acts of God," the Christian "story," there can be no finality about the language. Moreover, in dogma the thought is not discursive, but a direct apprehension of necessary implication; it is akin to what Proclus called the "perception of the soul" – ἐστί δὲ ψυχῆς αἴσθησίς τις.

I

With this background we may consider the doctrine of the Trinity. First, we must attempt to distinguish between the doctrine of the Trinity as theology and the doctrine as dogma. If, as has just been indicated, the distinction is not absolute, it is sufficiently clear. Thus theologians have disputed whether the Holy Ghost proceeds from the Father and the Son, or from the Father alone, or from the Son alone, or from the Father through the Son. This may be called a strictly theological question; it is concerned with the most adequate intellectual formulation of a religious apprehension. We can distinguish this from the religious apprehension itself. By the dogma of the Trinity I mean precisely that religious apprehension which leads the Christian to exclaim, "Glory be to the Father and to the Son and to the Holy Ghost, one God, blessed for ever!" It is not maintained that every Christian must use this particular formula, but that every Christian, in so far as he is a Christian, must mean what this formula expresses. To men of sound mind and Christian experience the meaning of the formula is, or may readily be made, intelligible. Indeed, while in theory we may attempt to distinguish substance from form, we may here recognize an instance where, so far as human language allows, substance coalesces with form. Further, it will be found that this religious or dogmatic expression of the Trinity is closely related to the " mighty acts of God " which constitute the Christian " story."

We must turn, therefore, to a more careful consideration of what is asserted in the doctrine of the Trinity. This doctrine was elaborated in the early centuries of the Christian faith, and has been unquestioned by the Church in later years. It has about it an element of finality, not because its complicated formulation and elaboration may not be improved, but because, as we shall see, as soon as Christians try to state their faith they are impelled by logic to some such formulation.

The doctrine of the Trinity points to a mystery, the Nature of the divine Being. Moreover, it is derived from the central Christian revelation, the Incarnation. How must we conceive of that Being whom we apprehend, not only as manifesting Himself through beauty and goodness, but also as bearing our sins and carrying our sorrows in Jesus Christ? The dogma of the Trinity is the necessary expression of *that* faith. Apart from faith in the miracle of the Incarnation, the religious (as opposed to the merely philosophical) doctrine of the Trinity is, of course, a largely unnecessary confusion of thought. Only as the necessary expression of the Word, the Gospel, the Incarnation, is the Trinity a dogma of the faith.

No exposition of the doctrine of the Trinity can make it simple; it constitutes a statement, not an explanation, of unfathomable mystery. Moreover, we are aware, again and again, in classical expositions of the doctrine that language becomes incoherent and breaks down in sad inadequacy to the thought it would express. Yet, apart from technicalities of thought, it is possible to make the doctrine intelligible to the educated reader.

A philosophical doctrine of true Personality in God

First, then, the doctrine is an assertion of true Personality in God. What do we mean by personality? We are psycho-physical organisms, and as human personalities are composed of the material and the spiritual. " We are only that amphibious piece between a corporal and spiritual Essence." But it is not beyond us to imagine disembodied personal spirits; therefore, though a bodily organism be necessary to the expression of our personality, we cannot say that a body is necessary to the idea of personality as such. In other words, personality is spiritual or non-physical. Further, we cannot conceive personality apart from mental life. But there cannot be a thinker without any thoughts. Thinking is the activity of the thinker, and thought its result. Moreover, we cannot conceive a thinker who had no emotional response whether of pleasure or pain in relation to his thoughts. Further, if his thoughts should include purposes, will is also implied; for purpose without the will, of which it is the purpose, is meaningless. I do not suggest that from a philosophical or psychological point of view this is a satisfactory account of personality, but at least it is intelligible; hence the doctrine of the Trinity, from the point of view from which we are now regarding it, may be made intelligible also.

(*Humble believers may skip to p.* 120)

If God is personal, the nature of His Personality cannot be identical with ours; but, if the term " personal " is to mean anything, His Personality must be analogous to ours. There must be in God something analogous to our thinking, willing, and feeling. Of these three the most difficult to ascribe to God is feeling, because with us feeling is so intimately bound up with our nerves, our senses, and our bodily structure. The early theologians of the Church were quite as conscious as are their modern critics that it is improper to describe God anthropomorphically. Yet they were convinced that God is personal, and therefore that personality in Him and in us must be analogous. Therefore they said that in God are three aspects or essential determinations, which they called the Father, the Word, and the Spirit.

We may for the moment paraphrase these names as standing for the subject of thought, the object of thought, and the relation between subject and object. Thus, to fall back on the human analogy, thought proceeds from the thinker; indeed the thinker generates his thought. Thus logically the thinker is prior to his thought; yet in fact there can be no thinker without any thought. A man's thought he articulates in a word; the word corresponds with the thought. But God is not as a man that He should grow in knowledge and gradually articulate His thought. His thought is eternal. Therefore it is said that He eternally generates His Word. But, as a man's thoughts are inseparable from the man himself, and, indeed, his thoughts are himself, so the Word of God is inseparable from God and is God; the Word is, to use philosophical terms, the object in the subject-object relation. As by a mental analysis we can distinguish a man from his thoughts, yet neither the man nor the thoughts can exist in separation from one another, so "the Word was in the beginning with God, and the Word was God." Further, since the verb, "generate" is proper to the dependence of the Word on the Father, we might substitute " Son " for " Word." If, however, the doctrine of the Trinity meant no more than this purely philosophical aspect of it now under discussion, the term " Son " would hardly have been used.

The Word, then, is the mind or thought or eternal purpose of God. It is, in Biblical language, the Wisdom of God. It is the Architect's Plan existing eternally in the mind of the Architect. It is the purpose and meaning of Creation and of all the works of Providence in Nature and in history. It is said in Scripture, that God by His Word or His Wisdom (the two terms are interchangeable) created and sustains the world. Finally, as Christians believe, the Mind and Purpose of God in the Creation and government of the world became concrete and embodied in Jesus Christ, the Word of God incarnate. It is because of the mysterious relation of Christ to the Word of God that the Word is appropriately called also " the Son."

The term " Spirit " is more obscure. The word originally means " breath." We may illustrate its use thus: two men, as we may imagine, are watching a distant view; they see something move, but it is wholly indistinct; at last one identifies the object; he can name it; a word is generated in his mind; this, however, he can only convey to the other by an explosion of breath in the utterance of the word. In some such sense the term Spirit is applied to God. His Word is His eternal purpose, His thought; but His thought includes Creation. Therefore it must be uttered. As the breath proceeds from a man's mouth and utters his thought, so, we read, the Spirit of God brooded over the chaos in the beginning and brought light and order. The Spirit expresses, therefore, the energy, the activity, the creative outgoing beyond Itself of Deity. If there is thought which includes purpose, there must be will. But, as we may say with equal propriety that the world proceeds from the mind of God or from His will, so we may equally ascribe Creation to the Word or to the Spirit. Thus the Spirit proceeds from the Father and from the Son, or from the Father through the Son.

But the term " Spirit " is used in a further sense more difficult to explain. St. Augustine says that the Spirit is the love of the Father for the Son, and of the Son for the Father – that is, the Spirit represents not merely an outgoing of Deity beyond Itself, but also an internal operation or relationship within the Godhead. This is difficult for us to grasp because, though we might be said to love our thoughts, our thoughts cannot by any possibility be said to love us. But this is because our thoughts are, as it were, the image of their object ; we do not create but only perceive the objects of our thought, or, if at any time we think not about real things, but about our own imaginations, we realize that we cannot give objective existence and actuality to these imaginations. We can give ideal but not real existence to the creatures of our mind. But it is necessary to conceive that God's thought is not receptive of impressions as is ours, for there is nothing other than God that can impress Him. Rather, God's thinking must be conceived as giving substance and actuality to that which He thinks. Therefore His thought, His Word, must be conceived as having subsistent being in itself. Hence His thought is both Himself and a real Other, and hence we may speak of a mutual love of the Father and the Word, and this mutual love itself must have subsistence while yet it is God Himself.

Beyond doubt this is intensely difficult, and we realize that we are seeking to express that which is utterly beyond our comprehension. But it is not mere word-spinning.

It is an attempt to state what is necessarily implied in the assertion that God is personal; for, if we deny that which here is so dimly asserted, we may be pantheists or atheists or philosophical absolutists or monists, but we cannot believe in a personal God.

How is all this related to dogma in the sense defined above? It is philosophy or theology; it is not dogma. It is not this intricate, abstract, and baffling theory which anyone must accept on peril of denying the faith. A dogma, it is true, lies behind it. In that revelation wherein we know God in His mighty acts, we know Him as the personal, active, redeeming God, our Father. It is, therefore, an integral element in the Christian faith that God is personal, because He is our Father. But the problem how we are to conceive of the Personality in God is a matter for theology, philosophy, and metaphysics; it is no part of the "story."

The God of the Christian "story," the God who "sent His Son," is personal. If anyone denied that God is personal, he would implicitly deny the story. Hence that God is personal is a necessary, permanent part of the substance of the faith. The intellectual interpretation of what it implies that we speak of God as personal belongs to the changing form of the faith. It would be surprising if all the philosophical enquiries into the nature of personality in recent years should not in the end help us to a better formulation than was possible sixteen hundred years ago. But it must for ever be a dogma that God is personal.

But is He not super-personal, say some. This is an impropriety of language rather than of thought. It is idle to speak of "super-personal" unless we can indicate wherein the "super" consists. That which exists may be personal or impersonal. What is meant by the assertion that God is super-personal is not that He is impersonal, but that, as compared with us, He is personal *sensu eminentiore*, in some more eminent way. This is properly expressed by saying that Personality in God is analogous to, but not identical with, personality in man.

II

The religious basis

So far, then, as we have attained at present, we should say that the doctrine of the Trinity is theology and is not dogma. We turn now from that which is almost entirely philosophical to that which is almost entirely religious.

The distinctive Christian revelation, as we have seen, is the Incarnation, the recognition that, in Jesus Christ, God has in some way condescended to our low estate and come amongst us. This apprehension illuminates not only the Figure of Jesus Christ but everything in our experience. We see now all things with new eyes; we have a new and better key wherewith to unlock our mysteries. There are two great mysteries – nature and history; and these two are but different aspects of the one mystery of evil. The modern man is almost obsessed with the problem of pain and suffering that comes from earthquake, flood, famine, and disease, and with the cruelties of that nature which he calls "red in tooth and claw." The Hebrews were much more oppressed with the problem of evil in history, the sufferings of the innocent, the triumphs of the tyrannical, the forces of cruelty and vengeance amongst men. Mankind would fain believe in the goodness of God, but nature and history seem to proffer one great question mark.

The first Christians had known God as the Creator and Sustainer of this enigmatic world. Now they had seen His glory in the suffering Redeemer, bearing the sins of men upon His heart and paying the debt of nature before His time upon the Cross. That of itself did not solve the intellectual problem of evil and of suffering; it may even have enhanced it. But in the apprehension of *God* in Jesus Christ there was necessarily involved the apprehension of the Creator and Sustainer of the world, the Lord of nature and of history. Violently, and of necessity, was the heresy of Marcion rejected; for he declared that the God of the Old Testament was not the God of the New, that the God of Redemption was not the God of Creation. It may be that all suffering takes on another hue when we remember that the Son of God has suffered; but in any case, as it is certain that Jesus Christ did not cut Himself off from the history and religion of His people, so the Church declared that the God it recognized in Jesus Christ was the God of Abraham and of the Fathers, the God who had spoken by the Prophets, the God of tempest and earthquake and volcano, and of the thin voice of silence. Therefore the Church in the very acceptance of Christ as the Incarnation of the Word of God declared that the God of Creation and the God of Redemption was One God blessed for evermore.

But, further, there was the experience of the Christian fellowship. This might be expressed in many ways, as that Christians knew that God had visited and had redeemed His people, or that the Kingdom had come, or that the Holy Ghost, promised for the last days, had been poured forth, or that they were translated out of darkness into the Kingdom of His dear Son, or that they were passed from death into life, or that they were in Christ, or that Christ was in them, or that they had received already eternal life, or that Christ was the Head and they the Body. The story of what had happened might be told in a thousand ways – the dogma is concerned with the concrete event, not with any particular description of it – but all descriptions declared in some form or other that the world in which the Son of Man had suffered was not the world as it had been before, that a new era had dawned, that the hand of the living God was still upon them as in the days of the Messiah, and that the God whom they had recognized in Christ they recognized anew in the breaking of bread and in the fellowship.

Thus, as a matter of religious experience, they apprehended God in three modes – Creator, Redeemer, Sanctifier, or Father, Son and Holy Ghost. Technically, and as thus stated, this is not the doctrine of the Trinity at all, for that doctrine asserts that God exists in three " Persons," not that we apprehend Him in three modes. This latter view is Modalism, a doctrine not of God's Being, but of our experience. But we are very near to the doctrine of the Trinity, because we could easily transpose this threefold apprehension into the form that we recognize God in three of His " mighty acts " – His Creation, His Coming, and His outpouring of the Holy Spirit. This at least is the experimental aspect or basis of the doctrine of the Trinity. In Nature, in Christ, and in the Church the Christian apprehends one God blessed for ever.

III

The Divine Being

But the doctrine of the Trinity is more than an assertion that God is Personal (there is nothing distinctively Christian in Theism), and more than the doctrine that we apprehend Him in three modes – Nature, Christ, and the Church (for that is a statement of our experience, not a doctrine of His Being). The doctrine of the Trinity is that God in His own essential Being is three " Persons " in one God.

It has always to be remembered that the doctrine of the Holy Trinity is a mystery, not an explanation, and that the mystery arises directly out of the Christian revelation. Theism in general has attempted to find a middle way between pantheism on the one side and deism on the other. Pantheism asserts that God is all and all is God. That is, it represents God as wholly immanent. Deism represents God as being as removed from His universe as the watchmaker from the watch that he has made; thus God is conceived as wholly transcendent. The God of pantheism of whom we are a part is not a God whom we can worship; the God of deism who stands remote from His Creation is not the God of religious experience. Hence a philosophy that would interpret the religious experience of poets and saints and seers and philosophers has always the task of representing God as both immanent and transcendent.

But the problem for Christian thought is more perplexing than this precisely where it is distinctively Christian. The Christian apprehends God as the transcendent Being, eternal and infinite, before all worlds, the Creator of all. He apprehends God likewise as in some sense immanent in the world which He sustains and orders. These two apprehensions are part of the religious inheritance from Judaism; they are given in the Christian experience (for the apprehension of God – that is, the Creator and Sustainer – in Jesus Christ the Redeemer is precisely the Christian revelation); and they may be established by strictly logical argument as by St. Thomas. For Christians, it is true, the problem of immanence seems to arise in a special form because God is apprehended as immanent in the Church in a sense in which He is not immanent in the world at large. But this distinction is intimately associated with the completely new and distinctive element in

The Incarnation and the Trinity

the Christian faith, that God comes to us Himself and " tabernacles amongst us " in Jesus Christ. The Christian, therefore, has to conceive of God as transcendent above history, as immanent in history, and in Jesus Christ as intrusive into history. It is because the Christian sees in Christ not merely a signal illustration of the immanence of God in history but the very coming of God himself into history that the Trinity which, as we shall see, is the expression of this apprehension, is the expression of the very essence of the faith. If in Jesus Christ we do not in some sense apprehend God Himself come amongst us, there is no need to produce a theological doctrine of the Trinity, there is no problem of Christology, and there is no Gospel, for there is no " story." We are left with a philosophy of religion and with a story of man, indeed, but no story about God.

This book is concerned with theology, not with apologetics. No attempt, therefore, is made to show that the Incarnation is a fact. What I desire to make clear is that the whole of Christian theology springs from and centres round the Christian revelation that Christ is in some sense " very God " as well as " very man," and that the denial of this fundamental revelation and dogma is the denial of the very heart of historic Christianity. This may be demonstrated by reference to the creeds and confessions. In the course of this exposition I have carefully and of set purpose used a very considerable variety of phrases for the expression of the Christian revelation (the Incarnation, the Coming of God, the sending of His only begotten Son and many others) ; no one formula is adequate, none explains the mystery, but the mystery itself is adequately denoted. He who understands any one of these phrases understands them all ; and he who has to tone them down or explain them away does not really accept the revelation. Much confusion has been introduced into theology in recent years by those who, claiming to restate the Christian faith, have taken some other starting-point than that which historic Christianity declares to be the Christian revelation.

What does the Incarnation mean? There are two questions here that can be distinguished but not separated. The first is, How are we to think of the Person of Jesus Christ? The second is, How are we to conceive of the Being of God? The first is dealt with under the heading of Christology, the second of the Trinity. It is with the second that we are now concerned.

In what language can we express the Christian revelation as it involves the Being of God? We cannot simply say, "God is Jesus" and "Jesus is God" – for two reasons: it is not sense to say without qualification that God, the Creator and Sustainer of the world, the eternal, immutable, infinite, and immaterial Being, *is* a particular baby lying on His Mother's knee, or *is* a human being hanging on a Roman Cross; second, if Jesus Christ were God simply, His human life was an appearance, not a reality; His prayers were play-acting; when He spoke of His Father, He meant Himself; He did not "with strong crying and tears" pray unto "Him that was able to save Him." In fact, to say, without qualification, "Jesus is God" is to deny the Incarnation, the Christian revelation, and has always been, therefore, strictly heretical.

Yet on the other hand the Christian revelation is not expressed but implicitly denied if we say that Jesus Christ was a man who in character and conduct was exactly like God; for the essence of the revelation is not that we learn what God is like but that we apprehend God Himself come for our redemption, or, to use the language of the Gospels, that God, who in times past had sent His servants the Prophets, sent at last His Son.

God in Three Persons

The doctrine of the Trinity does not solve this mystery, but it succinctly states it. God, it says, exists in three "Persons" – Father, Son, and Holy Ghost. The term "Person" here does not mean "person" at all in our ordinary sense of the word; it is the translation of the Latin word *persona*, which in this connection represents the Greek word *hypostasis*. The doctrine of the Trinity was formulated in Greek, and Person means what *hypostasis* means.

(*Humble believers may again skip without irreparable loss to the religious argument on p.* 128)

The meaning of hypostasis (*plural* hypostaseis)

There is unhappily no one English word that exactly corresponds with *hypostasis*, but its meaning can be indicated by two illustrations. First, all men share a common human nature, the possession of which constitutes them men. But there is no such thing as human nature in general; human nature only exists in separate, concrete, individual men. Here the concrete individual is the *hypostasis* in which the common nature subsists. The *hypostasis* is an individual, concrete, or subsistent determination of a common nature. The second illustration is taken from science, and will serve as an illustration, even though as a scientific statement it be defective. We say that water, when it boils, becomes vapour, and, when it freezes, becomes ice. There is, then, some common nature, *x*, which sometimes appears as water, sometimes as vapour, sometimes as ice. *x* is the common nature; water, vapour, and ice are its three *hypostaseis*, its three individual, concrete, or subsistent determinations, just as Peter and Paul and John and James and all other men are individual concrete or subsistent determinations of the common nature, "man." When, therefore, we say that God exists in three "Persons," we mean that God exists in three individual, concrete, or subsistent determinations of His nature.

Peter and Paul and James possess the same human nature, and possess it wholly ; each of them is a man with all the essential attributes of manhood ; but the three men are different from one another and eternally distinguishable. On the other hand, when we contemplate a particular human being, we distinguish the thinker from his thought, and both from the outgoing of his thought in will or feeling. We may say that the thinker is the man, or we may say that a man is what he thinks, or that a man is what he wills and feels. But while we distinguish the thinker, the object of his thought, and his will, we see that these three elements in the man have no separate existence ; they are not three *hypostaseis* (or individual concrete or subsistent determinations) of one common nature ; they are simply three aspects of one indivisible whole. When, therefore, we assert that God exists in three *hypostaseis* – the Father, the Word, and the Spirit – we are making the infinitely difficult assertion that in God there are those elements analogous to the thinker, the thought, and the will in man, that these three make up the one and indivisible nature of God, and yet that in Him the thinker, the thought, and the will are individual, subsistent determinations of His Being as distinct from one another as Peter from Paul.

Our difficulties are manifold. If the divine Being exists in three *hypostaseis*, we yet must avoid the assertion that there are three Gods. Conversely, we must say that the Word of God, which is the mind or purpose or plan or wisdom of God, has an individual subsistence of its own. The mystery is insoluble. Why, then, do we assert it ? We may offer two reasons, one philosophical, one religious.

A philosophical argument

We human beings are aware of ourselves only as over against that other which is not ourselves – that is, the world of our experience outside ourselves. We must conceive of God as personal – that is, as having in Himself something analogous to our consciousness. But God, whom we conceive as the Author and Ground of the universe, has no world of experience outside Himself by means of which He may be conscious. Therefore, unimaginable as this must be to us, He must be not only the subject but the object of His own "thought" and "experience." Further, as we have seen, whereas our thought is only reflective of reality, His thought must be conceived as constitutive of reality. In other words, that Other which is both Himself and the object of His thought must have concrete, actual subsistence. So, too, any outgoing of His Being whether in an act of will or in a mutual relationship between Himself and His Other must have actual subsistent being. For that which in us is, as we say, "purely mental" is imperfect, because it is a mere potentiality, not yet actualized. But it is not possible for us to ascribe to the supreme Being any imperfection; therefore we cannot ascribe to Him any potentiality that falls short of actuality. Therefore His thought and His will have substantial being. This is a brief and imperfect summary of a long metaphysical argument, but it will serve to indicate that there is philosophical justification, or even necessity, for the assertion that the Being of the one God exists in three *hypostaseis*.

A religious argument

We turn to the religious reason. It is of the essence of the Christian revelation stated in its simplest form that in Jesus Christ we see not merely a very good man, but God Himself come down for our redemption. In some sense we are compelled to say that Jesus Christ is very God Himself. We assert, not that, when Christ was born, God who hitherto had been the Author and Sustainer of the universe, the invisible eternal Being, suddenly ceased to be that and became instead a little child, but that we must offer to the little child that worship which we owe and pay to God alone. All the doctrine of the Trinity and of the " divinity " of Christ arises from the fact that Christ evokes our adoration and our worship, the same adoration and worship as we pay to God, which, indeed, we do pay to God as we pay it to Christ. Thus the Christian revelation itself involves that God exists in two *hypostaseis* – in the Father and in the Son – for the Son is both God and at the same time not the Father.

Further, the Christian revelation, as we shall see yet more clearly in a later part of this book, is not to be separated from the Church which is not only its custodian and its effect, but in a sense its actual continuance as part of that redemptive act (or series of acts) of God, the first chapter of which is recorded in the Old Testament, as the third chapter is recorded in the Acts of the Apostles. The Christian experience of God in Christ is distinguishable but not separable from the experience of God in the Church. I have already indicated several of the phrases which point to this latter experience – God has translated Christians out of darkness into the Kingdom of His Son; the Holy Spirit has been poured out upon them; they are in Christ; Christ is in the midst of them; He is the Head, they are the Body. The heterogeneity of the expressions manifests more clearly than could any one of them the nature of the underlying experience. It was a sense of the living Presence of God, not just as God is present in all His works, in the beauty of nature and the nobility of moral heroism. It was a presence of God in power, a presence as distinctive as the presence of the incarnate Word, a presence of God in the Spirit, so distinct from all previous experience that men could say that hitherto the Holy Spirit had not been given. What this involves in respect of the nature of the Church we must consider at a later stage. Enough for the moment that Christians were aware of God or of Christ in the fellowship of the Church as surely as they were aware of God in the historic Christ. God was with them in the Spirit. The Spirit was not the incarnate Christ, though it could not be separated from Him and might be called His Spirit. It was God's Spirit; but as a man's spirit is the man, yet is not identical with him, so God's Spirit is God Himself, yet not identical with the Father; it is God in a third *hypostasis*.

Thus is God known as one God in three Persons or *hypostaseis* – the Father, the Son, and the Holy Ghost. But how precisely is the Second Person of the Trinity identified with the historic Figure of Jesus Christ? We may say that the Holy Trinity is Father, Son, and Holy Ghost, or Father, Word, and Holy Ghost, but we may not say that it is Father, Jesus, and Holy Ghost. We shall come in the next chapter to the mystery of the Person of Christ, but we note here that in Christian theology Jesus Christ is not said to be God absolutely, nor the Word of God absolutely, but rather the Word incarnate.

The Word and the Spirit

But why is Jesus Christ said to be the Incarnation of the Word of God rather than of the Spirit of God? We distinguish God present in the flesh from God present in the Spirit; none the less, since the Holy Spirit is the Spirit of Jesus, Jesus Himself might not inappropriately be called the Incarnation of the Spirit. We may not pretend that our human language is adequate; but we can see that the misunderstanding that leads men to-day to speak so naturally of Him as the Incarnation of the Spirit is precisely the reason why He is not so called in orthodox theology.

In the course of the history of Christian thought it is inevitable that there has been confusion and ambiguity of terms. The Bible, in the beginning, speaks of the Spirit brooding over the chaos ; and the work of Providence in the ordering of the world is naturally ascribed to the Spirit of God. But there is the parallel Biblical conception that the world was formed by the Word of God, and that the instrument of God's Providence is His Word or Wisdom. Hence early Fathers could say that Christ as the Word (*Logos*) was known to the Old Testament Fathers, and was the agent of God in the providential ordering of history. Here the conceptions of Spirit and Word are indistinguishable. Thus, if we keep to the terms "Word" and "Spirit," it may be formally or theologically, but not spiritually or religiously, incorrect to speak of Him as God's Spirit incarnate. Yet the phraseology is to be avoided because, owing to an ambiguity of the term " Spirit " in this connection, many would assent to the doctrine that Jesus Christ is the Incarnation of God's Spirit who would deny what is meant by the assertion that He is the Incarnation of the Word.

Thus, when I spoke above of the religious grounds for the faith that the one God is known in three *hypostaseis*, the term " Spirit " was necessarily confined to the experience of the Church. When we mean by the Spirit that new life which was given at Pentecost, we distinguish the Spirit in this sense from the general providential government of the world by God ; we connect God the

Father with Creation and Providence, the Son with Christ, the Spirit with the Church. If, then, we were to say that Jesus Christ is the Incarnation of God's Holy Spirit, we might mean either that He was the Incarnation of that supernatural presence of God realized in the Christian fellowship, or that He was the Incarnation – that is, the embodiment or fulfilment or supreme and perfect achievement – of God's natural or normal working in Providence. In the former case we should be asserting the Christian revelation, in the latter, by implication, denying it; in the former case we should be using the word "Incarnation," in its proper sense of miracle and mystery, in the latter we should be using it in some metaphorical sense, as, for instance, when we say that Mr. So-and-so is the very incarnation of good manners. The Christian revelation is not that Jesus Christ is "the very incarnation of" God's Spirit, but that He is God Himself incarnate.

Some account has now been given of the meaning of the assertion that God is revealed as one God in three Persons, and of the experiential basis of this faith. But it has been maintained that Christian dogma is relative to "the mighty acts of God," the Christian "story." How, then, can the Trinity be Christian dogma?

The Trinity and the Gospel

The Christian "story" may be told in an indefinite number of ways, but essential moments in it are these: in the beginning God created the world; but man by his sin is alienated from God; God therefore undertook man's redemption; He sent His servants the prophets; but in the last days He sent His Son; His Son wrought man's redemption, and, through His life, death, and Resurrection, the Church, the new redeemed humanity, came into being; this was signalized by the outpouring of the Holy Spirit. That, in brief outline, is the "story." It centres round three "mighty acts" of God – the Creation, the Incarnation, the giving of the Holy Spirit. These three acts correspond not merely to three modes of our experience, but to three modes of the divine Being. Therefore the whole Christian "story" is epitomized in the triumphant declaration of the believing Church that Father, Son, and Holy Ghost together are worshipped and glorified, one God blessed for ever. Nor can any man deny this confession and accept the "story" which is the Gospel, the Christian revelation. The Trinity is the only all-comprehensive Christian dogma.

Chapter VII

THE HOLY NATIVITY

I

Are Christmas carols true?

MANY Protestants maintain a great love for Christmas carols, although in the singing of them they wonder whether they are being fully honest. They deny the affirmation of the creed, "conceived by the Holy Ghost, born of the Virgin Mary." Are they denying a dogma of the faith or correcting an historical misunderstanding? Are they repudiating the substance or a transient form of the Christian Gospel?

Various attempts have been made by learned apologists for the faith to prove that parthenogeniture, or birth from a single parent, is not impossible from the point of view of science. I am not able to appraise these arguments, but they do not seem to have been generally convincing, and it is a question whether they are even relevant. Is it necessary, is it possible, is it reasonable for us to-day to believe in "the Virgin Birth"?

The historical evidence

In part, at least, this is an historical question. What is the historical evidence that our Lord knew no human father? St. Mark, our earliest evangelist, makes no reference to the fact, and it is difficult to imagine why he kept silence if it was known to him, or to suppose that it was known to the primitive Church at large if it was unknown to him. No mention is made of the fact, if such it be, by St. Paul, our one contemporary authority; he alleges, indeed, that Christ was born "of the seed of

David" ; but, in view of the genealogies given by the first and third evangelists, this evidence might seem to tell against the Virgin Birth. The fourth evangelist tells of the Incarnation of the eternal Word, but without reference to this particular miracle. Indeed, in two passages (i. 45 and vi. 42), if our text is correct, he speaks of our Lord as the son of Joseph. Thus, apart from tradition, the only evidence for the Virgin Birth comes from St. Matthew and St. Luke. Even here the evidence is not all upon one side. The genealogy of our Lord is traced by both evangelists through Joseph. Further, it is alleged that only one verse in St. Luke's Gospel absolutely requires us to believe in a supernatural birth, and that various small indications in his narratives point to a different tradition.

Further, it is argued that the Virgin Birth cannot be isolated from the whole setting of the Nativity stories – the star, the magi, the flight into Egypt, the angels – which are obviously legendary in form and impossible to harmonise with one another.

It is small wonder, therefore, that many Christians have declared that they reject the story of the Virgin Birth with the whole cycle of Nativity narratives ; and it must be freely and frankly admitted that, apart from dogmatic considerations, the evidence for the Virgin Birth is not such as we could possibly expect the scientific historian to accept.

It may be replied that, if these stories are not true, some explanation of their origin must be offered, and that the conventional explanations from misunderstandings of Scripture and the comparative study of mythology are far from convincing. But the scientific historian may answer that our inability to explain the origin of these incredible stories does not make them credible. Many to-day would say that no amount of evidence would make them believe that Christ had no human father; and, on any showing, the evidence, it is alleged, is quite inadequate to make even arguable so stupendous a miracle.

Further historical objections are raised. If the Nativity stories are true, it is asked, how shall we account for the opposition or, at least, the misunderstanding of Christ's Mother later in His ministry? And what have the astronomers to say about the star? And how could the wise men identify a house in a village by a star in the sky? And what did the Lord's Mother do with the capital which was represented by the "wisers'" gifts? The extreme banality of some of these questions may be an indication that the whole setting of the enquiry is out of focus. Still, we cannot be surprised that an increasing number of Christians declare that they do not believe in the supernatural birth.

Is there any answer?

There was a time when the miraculous birth of Christ was a weapon in the hands of the apologist, who could argue that He must have been the Son of God because He was so born. We cannot adopt this line of argument to-day. It is not to be thought that any educated modern man will accept these stories unless he be a Christian. In other words, if the Virgin Birth can be proved, it will be on dogmatic, not historical, grounds.

Dogmatic considertions

We return, therefore, to the Christian revelation. The Christian apprehends in Jesus Christ, the Son whom God sent, the Word of God Incarnate, very God as well as very man. All these phrases, and others that might be quoted, are, as we have seen, attempts to indicate the Christian apprehension of a divine Condescension, a Coming of God

Himself into history, a new creative and redemptive act of God. The Christian believer, therefore, is not concerned, as the historian or scientist as such must be, with the question whether parthenogeniture is conceivable in the case of human beings generally; he is considering the coming into the world of the Incarnate Word, God's very Son. How can we say in advance that such an One must be born as we are with a human father? We are considering the birth of Christ, not human birth in general. From the believer's standpoint of faith the assertion of a miraculous birth presents no difficulty, if the evidence for it be sufficient. But is the evidence sufficient?

It is not infrequently argued to-day that, if Christians would abandon this legend of a supernatural birth, they would remove a serious stumbling-block in the way of the acceptance of Christianity. But this argument seems to rest upon a misapprehension. The removal of one miracle from the Christian story does not make the rest rational and credible. Those who plead this cause, therefore, usually proceed further. They would abandon the miraculous element from the Resurrection as from the birth, and would find a naturalistic explanation of the miracles narrated in the Gospels; thus ridding Christianity, as they suppose, of miracle, which is incredible to "the modern mind," they will be able to restate the faith in a manner acceptable and rational. But, unless not merely the argument of this book, but the New Testament itself, and the creeds and confessions of historic Christianity have misunderstood the essence of the faith which they exist to declare, the Christian revelation at its very centre asserts stupendous miracle – God's taking of our flesh, the Incarnation of the Word, the sending of His very Son. "Blessed is he that shall not be offended in Me."

He who is prepared to believe in the miracle of the Incarnation is not likely to be offended by the story of a supernatural birth.

But, if the Virgin Birth be no stumbling-block to faith, we still must ask if it is true. It must be admitted that the historical evidence of itself is insufficient; is the dogmatic evidence conclusive, or, in other words, is the Virgin birth implied in the Christian revelation, and is it thus a dogma of the faith?

Professor Brunner writes: "The doctrine of the Virgin Birth would have been given up long ago were it not for the fact that it seemed as though dogmatic interests were concerned in its retention. The first reason was this: it was argued that natural procreation is contrary to the divine significance of the Incarnation. Let us be quite clear on this point. The question is not: Is the birth of the Person of Christ a divine, saving miracle, the miracle of the Incarnation, or not? But it is this: Are we obliged to represent to ourselves the divine miracle of the Incarnation of the Son of God as a Virgin Birth or not? We are, namely, absolutely certain of the miracle of the divine fact. But that this miracle can be further explained by the addition of a biological factor, namely, development of life in the womb of the mother without male seed: the controversy rages round this biological interpretation of the miracle. Our double thesis is this: firstly, the divine miracle does not permit us to offer detailed explanations; the fact itself should be enough for us; the way in which it happened is God's secret. Secondly, the Son of God assumed the whole of humanity; thus He took on Himself all that is human, all that lies within the sphere of space and time. Procreation through the two sexes forms part of human life. It is a process in time and space; we can know whether it has taken place or not apart from faith. If we do not know about it, this has nothing to do with faith at all; it simply constitutes a gap in our knowledge."

It is impressive that Dr. Brunner, who is as far removed as possible from being an unbeliever or even a modernist, declares that the doctrine of the Virgin Birth is really inconsistent with the very miracle which it is supposed to illustrate; for, unless Christ had a human father as well as a human Mother, he did not really assume our nature. πάντα ἀνέλαβεν, ἵνα πάντα ἁγιάσῃ – He assumed all that He might sanctify all.

Dr. Brunner is critical of the traditional doctrine of the Two Natures in Christ, because, he says, "a miracle of salvation is turned into a metaphysical problem." But, if we cannot follow Dr. Brunner and his school in their depreciation of metaphysics, and if we were to accept the traditional christological doctrine of the Two Natures, would the Virgin Birth be necessarily implied? I write with hesitation, but I think not. The traditional orthodox doctrine, as we shall see, is that the divine Word assumed a human body, a human soul, a human mind (but not a human personality). I see no logical objection to the view that he received from human parents His human body, soul, and mind.

Is the Virgin Birth a dogma?

Is, then, the Virgin Birth a dogma of the Christian faith? It is a dogma in the Roman sense, because it is stated in Scripture and defined as a dogma by the Church. It is not, however, a dogma in the sense defended above. It is not a dogma unless it can be shown to be given or necessarily implied in that apprehension of God in Christ which is the Christian revelation. It is necessary to the "story" which is the Gospel that the Word became flesh, but the particular manner of His coming into the world (regarded as a physiological event) is not an integral part of the story. The physiological element in the assertion "conceived by the Holy Ghost, born of the Virgin Mary" is not to be logically derived from, nor is it given in, the apprehension of God in Jesus Christ.

I do not myself think that the arguments by which theologians have sought to prove that the Incarnation implies the Virgin Birth are conclusive. But, if the necessary logical connection of the two conceptions could be demonstrated, the Virgin Birth would become a dogma, and the miraculous nature of the biological event and the intrinsic insufficiency of the historical evidence would be irrelevant. If the Incarnation implies the Virgin Birth, then all who believe the former must believe the latter; and the only reason for denying that the Virgin Birth is a *dogma* is precisely the failure of the demonstration that it is implied *inevitably* in the Incarnation.

When it is said that the Virgin birth is not a dogma, however, the denial must be strictly limited to that which to-day is taken to be the meaning of the phrase "Virgin Birth." That is to say, if the words of the creed, "conceived by the Holy Ghost, born of the Virgin Mary," be understood to be the assertion of a particular miracle in the sphere of biology, then the assertion of that particular physiological wonder is not of the essence of the Christian Gospel; it may be questioned without involving a questioning of the faith.

There can, of course, be no doubt but that the framers of the creeds supposed themselves to be implying a biological miracle, for the Scriptural tradition was unquestioned by them; but it is another question whether, when the biological miracle has been asserted, we have grasped the central significance of the clause, " conceived by the Holy Ghost, born of the Virgin Mary." Granted that the creed intends here that the Lord had no human father, is this all that the creed intends, or even the most important part of it ? The Nicene Creed, in its fuller and more poetical phraseology, declares our faith in the only-begotten, consubstantial Son, " who for us men, and for our salvation, came down from heaven, and was incarnate by the Holy Ghost of the Virgin Mary, and was made man." It is the assertion that the Word took flesh, that the Son of God has come down to earth.

Is the Incarnation an historical event ?

This, beyond all question, is the essence of the Christian " story," the marrow of the Gospel, the proclamation of unfathomable mystery, the miracle of miracles. But is it an historical event ? This, again, in the form in which we put it is a modern subject, for the scientific study of history is a recent achievement. We do not call Herodotus a scientific historian in our modern sense, and Thucydides was a philosopher who wrote the history of his own time to be a mirror for all times. Even yet we have hardly realized, as much New Testament scholarship shows, what complexity is introduced into our subject by the canons of scientific history. Thus Bertheim, in his great book on the methodology of history, says : " It is the fundamental axiom of all historical knowledge that human nature is always one and the same." History is concerned with men, their deeds, their thoughts, their habits, their institutions, and their culture. History does not deal with animals except in their relations with men ; still less can history deal with fauns or centaurs or the creatures of fable ; even less can God be a subject of historical enquiry. But it is of the essence of the Christian revelation that Jesus Christ is in some sense God Himself ; He is " very

God" as well as "very man," the Incarnate Word. How, then, can historical canons be applied to Him?

This question bears closely upon our next chapter concerned with the doctrine of the Person of Christ. We must answer for the moment that, since believers and unbelievers are agreed that our Lord had a human body and soul and mind, He is a subject of historical enquiry. If, as Christians believe, He was also the Son of God, the incarnate Word, the Incarnation involved some kind of "incognito" such that all men could see the purely historical, but the eyes of many were holden that they could not see His glory. Now, the coming into the world of the Son of God is an historical event, for the Incarnation means that the divine entered history. But it is also a meta-historical or super-historical event, since it was a "mighty act" of God, and, as we have seen, it is man's acts, not God's, which are the subject of history. While, therefore, the Incarnation is an historical event, it is also a super-historical event – an act of God; it marks the moment where the infinite crosses the finite, the eternal the temporal. If the birth of our Lord, therefore, be recorded merely as an historical event, it is misrecorded, for its distinctive element is omitted.

This is the fundamental significance of the Nativity stories. Their truth lies precisely in this, that they represent His birth not only as an historical event, but also as more than an historical event. His birth is indeed the coming of a little child to a human Mother, but it is also the coming of God Himself, His condescension to our low estate. If, therefore, we should say, "The birth of our Lord was just like any other human birth, and we reject the tales of His Nativity," we should be much further from the truth than if we made the mistake of confusing prose and poetry. We should be much further from the truth – our rejection of the Nativity stories might be the necessary way of stating all the historical and scientific truth about His coming, but the Incarnation of the Word is much more than an historic and scientific fact; it is the act of God. Because it is the act of God, we have no language adequate for it; we can only use the language of picture, of symbolism, of story; nor could human language more perfectly express the meaning and spiritual reality of His coming than is done in the stories of the Nativity. If, therefore, we ask, after the fashion of children, "Are these stories true?" the answer is, "Yes, they are true." Their truth, indeed, is not like the formal adequacy and correctness of a textbook on law or chemistry, but they are true because they declare the Incarnation of the Word of God. They are a true statement of the spiritual facts; they are true to the "story" – they *are* the story, though, as we learn from St. Paul and St. John, the story may be told in other terms. So regarded, the Nativity stories are not in any essential regard the proclamation of a miracle in the field of biology; they are a statement of the point where the eternal crosses history and God is made man. "Conceived by the Holy Ghost, born of the Virgin Mary" is by no means the only possible formulation of the Christian dogma, but it is at least one of the ways in which the mystery of the Incarnation may not unfittingly be set forth.

We are not unaccustomed to questions to which a plain answer of "Yes" or "No" cannot be given. Do I believe that the first chapter of Genesis is true? Certainly I do. That chapter declares that in the beginning God created the heavens and the earth. That, as we have seen, is a dogma of the Christian faith. But I am sure that the chapter does not give a scientifically accurate picture of the cosmic process. As a scientific statement, therefore, I could not accept that chapter as wholly true. Do I believe the Nativity stories – that angels heralded the birth of Christ; that wise men led by a star brought Him their gifts and adoration; that shepherds worshipped Him; that the ass knew his Owner and the ox his Master's crib? Most certainly I do. But are the statements historically accurate? How could they be? For they are, in essence, expressions of the super-historical aspect of that which also was an event in history.

II

The Virgin Mother

There could be no clearer indication of the tragic corruption into which the Church had fallen before the Reformation than the indignation and fury with which so much was cast aside. The cult of the Virgin Mother was utterly repudiated by the Protestants, so much so that to this day I suppose a Protestant minister is hardly ever to be found to preach from the text: "Hail, thou that art highly favoured; the Lord is with thee: blessed art thou among women." In the next chapter we come to the doctrine of the Person of Christ. We may conclude this chapter with a consideration of His Mother.

The Mother of God

One of the great theological battles of the Early Church was epitomized in the discussion whether or not the title Theotokos, Mother of God, might be properly ascribed to the Holy Virgin. No Protestant thinks of calling her the Mother of God, but do Protestants agree with the heretic Nestorius? Alternatives were suggested: let her be called Christotokos, said some; for no one could deny that she was in fact Christ's Mother. Let her be called

Theophoros, said others, for assuredly she carried God with her. The Church did not deny the propriety of these alternatives, but declared, with passion, that she is Theotokos, Mother of God.

Why was the Church dissatisfied with the term Christotokos, Mother of Christ? For two reasons, which are only formally distinct. First, Mother of Christ might be taken as a purely historical description of her office; she was, as a matter of fact, the Mother of Him who is called Christ. Second, the title might be taken to mean, and was intended by Nestorius to mean, that she was not the Mother of God – that is, the Mother of One who was very God as well as very man. Nestorius, indeed, fell far short of the negations to which we have grown accustomed; he was remote indeed from being what we call a Unitarian; his heresy, which lay in saying that after the Incarnation Christ was not both God and man having divine and human nature, but a Being composite and neither truly God nor truly man, might seem to many to-day at worst an aberration in theology. But the Church held it vital to assert that in Christ we meet, not with a supernatural Being, half God, half man, but with very God Himself in the fulness of the Godhead. However remote some of the discussions may seem to us, and however unconvincing some of the arguments of the orthodox, and however far the orthodox Church was from a sympathetic understanding of what Nestorius personally meant and believed, we can see now that the Church was insisting on the very essence of the Christian revelation, the apprehension of God Himself in Christ, when it insisted that the Virgin should be called Theotokos.

We can see the issue yet more plainly in regard to the term Theophoros, or "she who carries God." For this is open to two interpretations. It might, indeed, mean "she who carries God in her womb," but, were this meant, there could be no possible objection to calling her also Theotokos – "she who brought God to birth." Therefore, in fact, the term Theophoros means the God-carrying one, in the sense of the God-filled one or the God-inspired one. The objection to this was that, as any true Christian might be called Christophoros (or Christopher) because wherever he goes he brings Christ with him, so any holy person might be called Theophoros – one who brings God. Thus the title Theophoros did not state, and was intended to deny, precisely that which Theotokos asserts – that she was the Mother of Him who being man was also God. I do not suggest that Protestants are called to speak of the Virgin Mary as Mother of God, yet this ancient title is an epitome of the Christian faith; like the term "Incarnation" itself it involves the whole of the Christian revelation and nothing else.

"Ecce ancilla Domini"

Who, then, was she? It is not surprising (however regrettable it may be) that in view of her inconceivable prerogative, men should have dreamt of her Immaculate Conception and crowned her as the Queen of Heaven. Much of the cult of Our Lady has been developed since the Reformation, and one may, perhaps, blame Protestants in part for this, for they did not see that she more than any might be regarded as the patron saint of the Protestant Confession.

This is no mere paradox. The Roman Church, in spite of St. Augustine and St. Thomas, has been deeply tinged with semi-Pelagianism. The sheer grace of the sacraments has been counterbalanced or supplemented by the merits of the saints. In reaction from this, Protestantism has emphasized, perhaps to the point of exaggeration, the impossibility of any human merit and the sole sovereignty of God. So inconceivable has seemed the prerogative of the Holy Mother that in 1854 the Roman Church declared, not merely as a theological conclusion, but as a formal element in the deposit of faith – that is, as an essential dogma of revelation – that the blessed Virgin Mary at the first moment of her conception was miraculously immune from every taint of original sin. Thus she becomes the supreme illustration of virtue, not of grace.

Protestants have naturally paid slight attention to a doctrine which lacks all the marks of catholicity. Nothing in Scripture suggests that the Mother of the Lord was anything but a normal – that is a fallen – human being. If the biological miracle of a Virgin Birth is not necessarily implied in the Christian Gospel, still less is the Immaculate Conception of the Saviour's Mother. The doctrine of the Immaculate Conception represents the miracle that a human Mother bore the Incarnate Word, but, as I shall suggest, it mistakes the nature of that miracle.

It was by faith, and faith alone, that according to Scripture the Virgin Mary was able to be the Mother of the Lord. *Ecce ancilla Domini* – "Behold the handmaid of the Lord ; be it unto me according to thy word." Like the salvation of every one of us it is impossible, but "be it unto me according to thy word." Abraham has been called the Father of the faithful because he hoped against hope and believed the impossible and trusted in the naked Word of God ; and the Virgin Mary may be so called the Mother of the faithful because she said, "Be it unto me according to thy word." The good news is that God is He "that justifieth the ungodly" ; so God is He who made a human Mother able to bear the Son of God. Therefore to God alone is all the glory.

The pious imagination of Christians may seek to enter into the mind of the Mother of the Lord, but the sober prose of theological discussion must be hushed to silence. Blessed indeed is she among women, and glorified is all womanhood in her. The mystery of her Motherhood is summed up in those two phrases, which are the trumpet calls of the Reformation: "*Sola fide*" and "*Soli Deo gloria*" – "By faith and faith alone" and "To God alone be glory."

CHAPTER VIII

"AND WAS MADE MAN"

I

The Divinity of Christ the starting-point

"AND was made man" – this is another of the phrases that point to the heart of the Christian revelation. The reader will bear in mind that my definition of the Christian revelation is not arbitrary or subjective. I have not defined the revelation by what I happen to "feel" or happen to believe. The Christian revelation appears to the non-believer a self-deception. Those who well know what it is to doubt can have much sympathy with the non-believer, but they cannot have much sympathy with those who virtually deny the Christian revelation and then set forth their unbeliefs as a restatement of the Christian faith.

We may say that, in general, the Christian revelation takes three forms of expression. First, in the Synoptic Gospels it is in the form of a declaration of the advent of the heavenly Kingdom brought by the Son of Man and of the New Covenant "in His blood." Second, in the rest of the New Testament it is in the form of embryonic theology or illustration centring round the Church and the significance of Him who was the Son of Man; thus for St. Paul He is "the Second Adam," the Head of the Church, the pre-existent Son of God, who, "being in the form of God," took "the form of a servant," and who reconciled us to God "by the blood of His Cross"; for St. John He is the Word of God Incarnate; in the last book of the New Testament He is the "Lamb slain from the foundation of the world." The difference between these two modes of expression lies chiefly in the fact that between the sayings of the Lord " in the flesh " and the writings of the first apostles there lie the Cross, the Resurrection, and Pentecost. The third mode of presentation is in the more formal definitions of the Church which assert that Jesus Christ was " very God " and " very man." The revelation or Gospel, as has been stated again and again in these pages, can be expressed in an indefinite number of ways and in none perfectly and finally. But all modes of expression point to a " mighty act of God," an act of unique and saving Condescension on the part of Deity. That this is the heart of the Christian Gospel is demonstrable to all except those who, consciously or unconsciously rejecting the revelation, are determined to claim for their thought the name of Christian.

Thus the words, " and was made man," like Theotokos, define in a phrase the essence of the revelation. If we do not believe the revelation, there is no problem of Christology – that is, no problem of the Person of Christ – except in so far as every man of genius is a " problem." In place of the old question of how God became man, we have only to consider how man became God, that is, how One who was not God came to be called God. The acceptance of what is popularly called "the divinity of Christ " is the starting-point of Christian theology. By this is not meant that we must start theologizing with some formula of definition accepted on authority, but rather that we must start from the Christian revelation, and that this revelation itself, on its subjective side, is the adoring recognition of very God come for our salvation in Jesus Christ. This, as I say, is demonstrable from the New Testament and the history of Christian thought and piety.

The fact does not in any degree depend upon whether the writer or the reader of this book acknowledges the revelation.

Very God and very Man

Thus the problem of this chapter and of Christology in general is not whether Jesus Christ is "divine," not even whether the phrase "very God and very man" expresses a dogma of the Church, but how we may best express in terms of thought that which we apprehend in revelation or "experience." In other words, does the Christian revelation involve the teaching which comes to us with all the authority of traditional Christianity, that, as the Deity is Three Persons in one God, so Jesus Christ has Two Natures (the divine and the human) in one Person?

The formulation of the doctrines of the Trinity and of the Person of Christ was the great theological achievement of the early centuries. Can we deny the doctrine that Jesus Christ was very God and at the same time very man without denying the Christian revelation? And, if we make this affirmation, can we attach any conceivable meaning to it?

Both parts of the Christian affirmation have been repudiated; it has been denied that He was man, as it has been denied that He was God. There have been those who have said that, though He looked like a man and could be mistaken for a man, His manhood was appearance only, not reality; His humanity was but a dress which divinity assumed. This is the subtle heresy to which believers often have been tempted. It must be decisively rejected as inconsistent with the Christian revelation; for the Christian revelation is precisely this, that we apprehend God Himself in Him who really hungered and thirsted, really suffered, really died, really walked by prayer and obedience and faith.

The virtual denial of "very God"

Similarly it has been denied that Jesus Christ was God. The denial is substantial rather than formal, for it is recognized by all Christians that in some sense Jesus Christ is divine; but in what sense? We often quote the line of Whittier: "Jesus divinest when Thou most art man." I have myself often in the past quoted it with approval as indicating a conception of His divinity much more credible than that of the old-fashioned doctrine. The saying suggests that Jesus Christ is to be recognized as one with God, not because of His divine metaphysical nature, but precisely because of those human qualities of mercy, of kindness, and of love wherein He mirrors the heart of the Father. The same view may be put in another way: man, it is said, was made in the image of God; there is, therefore, in all men, a likeness to God, a spark of the divine; but, whereas in the case of most men this divine image is worn away and hidden, as is the king's head on a much battered and bespattered coin, in Christ's case the image is clear and perfect as is the king's head on a coin new issued from the Mint.

This conception may be developed in either of two ways. First, it may be said that our Lord is called divine, because He is in character wholly *like* the Father. But in this case He may only be called God in the same sort of way that we may say that Nelson's statue in Trafalgar Square is Nelson. Second, it may be said that, since man was made in the image of God, there is not an absolute distinction between God and man; man may approximate to God in varying degrees; further, every good man, in so far as he is good, is a revelation of God, and, more, every good man, in so far as he is good, is God's gift to mankind; therefore in Jesus Christ, the perfect man, we have at once the supreme revelation of God and God's supreme gift to man. Man, in fact, ascending to the perfection of his manhood, touches heaven and is one with God.

Some thought along these latter lines is common to-day, and often represents a sincere attempt to explain (and not to explain away) what is meant in the Christian confession by the " divinity " of Christ. None the less, it is a real, even if also an unintentional, denial of the Christian dogma that Jesus Christ is very God as well as very man. It is true that our Lord is represented as the gift of God to us, but only in the sense in which in a much less degree all good men, and, indeed, all good things, are of God's gift to us. This doctrine misses the heart of the matter because it fails to give expression to the divine initiative and Condescension. It might be summed up in the form that God, who aforetime spake by the Prophets, hath in these last days evoked or evolved His Son. Or, to put the objection in another form, this doctrine, that Jesus Christ as perfect man is thereby " divine," bears no relation to the dynamic and cataclysmic teaching of the Gospels concerning the advent of the supernatural Kingdom, of the Son of Man, and of the New Covenant " in His blood." Or, again, this view gives no place for the Christian conviction that we are not redeemed by man, even by the perfect man, but by the " mighty act " of God. There is no humility of the Incarnation here, no uttermost Condescension, no rending of the heavens that God Himself may come to seek and save the lost. This doctrine, therefore, if not in form or in intention, yet in fact is a denial of the Christian revelation.

There are in the main three ways according to which in times past the doctrine of Christ's Person has been set

The Adoptionist view

forth – the Adoptionist, the Kenotic, and the classical. The Adoptionist view is that there was a man, Jesus of Nazareth, whom God chose and exalted to be Messiah and His Son. Our Lord, in fact, is a deified man. We need not linger upon this, for it must by now be plain that this fails to represent the Christian revelation. The movement is from earth to heaven, not from heaven to earth. This is no equivalent of, " God sent His Son " ; this is not the Incarnation, the Christmas message.

The Kenotic view

The Kenotic view is based upon the passage where St. Paul says that Christ, being in the form of God, " emptied Himself " and took upon Him the form of a servant. The Incarnation is represented as a self-emptying of God. Thus it is said that God emptied Himself, in some part, of the use of His omnipotence and His omniscience, that He might walk the earth as Man. The real objection to this view is not that it denies, but that it does nothing to illuminate the Incarnation. It is put forward as an alternative to the classical or traditional doctrine, but it is rather a phrase than a doctrine ; if it were to be worked out, either it would be put in a form akin to that of classical Christology, or else it must in some way deny the true and real humanity of Christ.

The classical doctrine

We come, then, to the traditional doctrine of His Person. We must not expect to find here an explanation of the mystery of the Incarnation, nor is it to be suggested that a final or completely satisfactory statement of the implications of the Christian revelation is to be found in it. Our question is, not whether the Incarnation is a dogma of the faith, but whether the doctrine that Christ has Two Natures in one Person is a dogma as is the doctrine that God is Three Persons in one God.

II

A word of personal confession may be permitted. Through many years I confidently asserted that, whatever form the doctrine of the Person of Christ might ultimately take, the traditional (Chalcedonian) ascription to Him of two Natures in one Person must be abandoned. My reasons for this attitude were twofold: first, it seemed to me that a Being having a divine mind and a human mind, a divine will and a human will, is to-day inconceivable in view of our modern psychological knowledge; I conceived, then, that some sort of dual personality was involved. Second, under the influence of Herrmann, I supposed that the Two Natures doctrine in fact contradicted the Nicene faith and the deepest apprehension of the Christian that we meet with God in the man Christ Jesus. Both these objections, as I now suppose, rest upon a misunderstanding.

According to the classical expression of the Christian faith, then, we say that Christ was truly man, but not that He was *a* man; there was no man, Jesus of Nazareth, to whom was added divinity. Christ, we say, assumed human nature, but not a human personality. This is a point so baffling to modern readers that it must be expounded at some length.

Original Sin

The Two Natures doctrine logically presupposes the doctrine of Original Sin.[1] This latter doctrine is popularly understood thus: Adam is taken to have been the father of the whole human race; according to the legend in Genesis, Adam sinned; it is supposed, then, that his

[1] To theologians the insertion of a disquisition on "original sin" into a Christological chapter will appear strange. My excuse is that the current doctrine of the "divinity" of Christ is often in terms of the "divinity of a human saint or prophet."

sinfulness, his fallen human nature, has been transmitted to all his posterity in natural generation. All the race, therefore, is involved in Adam's fall, Adam's guilt, and Adam's penalty. The only way of escape from our *damnosa hæreditas* is through faith in Christ, which is signified in baptism. Unbaptized infants, therefore, when they die inherit hell. Because this does not commend itself to the mind and conscience of men to-day, "Original Sin" has been totally denied. It is not to be maintained that the destination of unbaptized children to hell is given in the Christian revelation of the Incarnation, nor can we logically derive from the revelation the mode in which human sinfulness is transmitted from generation to generation. It is very obvious, then, that if the old doctrine of Original Sin contains a truth of revelation, this is a case where substance must be distinguished from form.

Not a few have abandoned the doctrine altogether on two main grounds – one that the Fall of man is pure legend, not an historical event; the other that, when the Lord said concerning children that "of such is the Kingdom of Heaven," He declared once for all the innocence and purity of children.

We may consider the second reason first. When the Lord said that the Kingdom is of such as are little children, we may not lightly infer that little children are in no need of forgiveness and of a Saviour, unless we also understand Him to mean that the Kingdom is of those who need no forgiveness and no Saviour.

More serious is the contention that the Fall of man is not an historical event. Some would say that the discovery of Evolution has made the Fall of man an impossible conception. This, I suppose, is to misunderstand or misapply the scientific doctrine of Evolution. There is plenty of evidence which connects our bodily structure with the rest of animal nature, and few would wish to question that physical Evolution which, I understand, is epitomized in the history of the human embryo. But no science and no evidence would indicate that what we call "self-consciousness" is evolved by gradual stages from that which, so far as we know, is without "self-consciousness"; no one has successfully derived man's sense of moral obligation from anything amoral, and there is nothing to show that man is more religious now than he was before the dawn of history. The natural sciences have nothing to say about the Fall or the Evolution of man as a moral or spiritual event.

It need scarcely be said, however, that we cannot take the story of Adam and Eve, of the serpent and the "apple," as authentic and scientific history. If the Fall be an event, it can hardly be an historic event but, rather, it must be prehistoric or super-historic in the sense that human history does not begin till after the Fall. This is implied in that saying of Bertheim, quoted above, that the identity of human nature is the fundamental axiom of all historical enquiry. If human nature is fallen, it is only with fallen human nature that history deals; therefore the Fall is not an event within human history.

But, if we abandon the hopeless attempt to show that the Fall is an event of scientific history, and if we abandon the theory, which has no Scriptural authority, that the sin of Adam is transmitted by physical generation, we are in a position to recognize the spiritual fact which corresponds with the doctrine. This is not, as some have supposed, the merely empirical fact that there is actually to be found no sinless person (Christ usually excepted); rather, it is the spiritual fact that we cannot help being sinners, that we are born to sin, and that no struggles on our part can make us sinless. In any particular situation, no doubt, we are usually free to refrain from doing what we know to be wrong, but part of the burden we bear is that our thoughts are wrong, our desires are wrong, our ideals are wrong – at least in large measure. A little child is in its own implicit thought the centre of the universe; all things and all persons must minister to its imperious will; only very gradually is obedience learnt and patience and thoughtfulness for others. We start life with the centre of our interest on ourselves; but goodness consists in this – that the centre of our love is shifted from ourselves on to God and our neighbour. If all my thinking has a self-reference, I cannot lose the self-reference by more thought and thus save myself. The perversion of sin has been admirably put by Archbishop Temple in his recent Gifford Lectures: "The centre of trouble is not the turbulent appetites, though they are troublesome enough, and the human faculty for imagination increases their turbulence. But the centre of the trouble is the personality as a whole, which is self-centred and can only be wholesome and healthy if it is God-centred. This whole personality in action is the will; and it is the will which is perverted. Our primary need is not to control our passions by our purpose, but to direct our purpose itself to the right end. It is the form taken by our knowledge of good and evil that perverts our nature." (Dr. Temple means that we take that to be good which is not really good, being led astray from the true good by the apparent good.) "We know good and evil, but we know them amiss. We take them into our lives, but we mis-take them. The corruption is at the centre of rational and purposive life. . . . We totally misconceive alike the philosophic and the practical problem of evil if we picture it as the winning of control over lawless and therefore evil passions by a righteous but insufficiently powerful reason or spirit. It is the spirit which is evil; it is reason which is perverted; it is aspiration itself which is corrupt." It is this universal and necessary sinfulness which lies behind the saying of the Lord, "If ye then, being evil . . ."

It will be seen that this "original sin" is to be distinguished from "sins" in the sense of deliberate acts which violate our conscience; and it will be recognized that, if man was made in the image of God, it is not improper to speak of our "fallen" human nature. So understood is "original sin" a dogma, or, in other words, is it included or implied in the Christian revelation?

The Word of God, as we have seen, is in the first instance a revelation of God Himself in Jesus Christ, but it is also a light which enables us to see all life with new eyes. In the light of Jesus Christ we know ourselves and all men to be sinners. How can we possibly know *all* men to be sinners, since the number of men we know is very limited? Because we see that from our earliest days we have had wrong and unworthy thoughts of God, we have not loved Him with all our strength and mind and soul, we have not loved our neighbour as ourselves, we have constantly desired that which was not desirable and aimed at that in which our true good did not lie; our will, our thought, our desire have been perverted; and, while there is very much for which we blame ourselves, we cannot hold ourselves personally responsible for all; for much goes back to our training, our environment, our inevitable misunderstanding. We recognize that to have always thought and willed and acted and felt aright was impossible for us; it would have been "against human nature." It is not as particular sinners, but as human beings that we are subject to " original sin " ; therefore what we know of ourselves we know of all human beings ; " original sin " belongs to " fallen " human nature. The sinfulness and impotence of man which necessitated and called forth the mighty redeeming act of God are implicit in the Christian revelation itself. Therefore " original sin " and the Fall, not the phrases, but their substance, belong to the essence of the faith ; they are strictly dogmas of the secondary order – that is, they are not descriptions of the " mighty acts " of God, but are implicit in the Christian " story " ; for the Christian " story " cannot be told except in some such form as this – that because man was lost in sin and darkness and could not save himself, therefore God sent His Son.

" Original sin," then, is a dogma ; human nature is " fallen." What, then, do we mean by the clause in the creed, " and was made man," or by " the Incarnation " ? Do we mean that the Son of God assumed fallen human nature and became a sinner in need of redemption like the rest of us ? No, for how could He save us if He shared our mortal weakness ? Further, it is of the essence of the revelation that in Jesus Christ we meet not with a fellow-sinner, but with God Himself.

Therefore we say that the Word assumed human nature, but not fallen human nature ; He became man, but not *a* man ; He took our flesh, but not a human personality.

III

Human nature

What precisely do we mean by " human nature " ? The early Fathers spoke of a human body, a human soul, a human mind ; we may define it if we will, as a human psycho-physical organism. This is what is meant when it is said that in the Incarnation the Word of God assumed our human nature.

We must now return to the word *hypostasis*, which we discussed in connection with the Holy Trinity. Human nature is shared by all human beings, and has no existence of its own apart from the human beings who possess it. That is, human nature exists only in its *hypostaseis*, its concrete individual determinations. Human nature is everywhere the same; the differences between human beings, then, are not differences in their human nature, but in their individual particularity, their *hypostasis*. Peter and Paul and John and James and all other men are different *hypostaseis*, different concrete individuals who manifest a common human nature.

Using current phraseology, I have written above of "fallen human nature" to indicate "original sin" or the common moral disease of the race. But the "Fall" here is a spiritual, not a physical, matter; so far as our physical constitutions are concerned, the scientists may be right in denying the "Fall"; further, in so far as man is personal, a rational creature, he is "made in the image of God." In the sense, then, in which we are now using the term "human nature" – that is, of human body, human soul, and human mind, or of the human psycho-physical organism – human nature is morally neutral and may not be called "fallen." The term "nature" is not really being used in two senses. Human nature comprises the human body, the human powers of thought, the human psychological framework which are ours. These are a good gift; the body is adequate to express and serve the spirit; there is nothing in our human endowment which compels us to think and feel wrongly; human nature is good. Yet are all men caught in the meshes of ignorance, prejudice, false judgment, self-deception, and pride ; by the grace of God we may, perhaps, be delivered from these infirmities, but we must inevitably have shared them with all our fellow-mortals in greater or less degree. This is what is meant by " original sin," and our fallen human nature. " Original sin " is due not to our deliberate choice of evil, but to the fact that we are not mere individuals, but members of families and of societies, and that from our earliest days we imbibe lessons of false judgment concerning God and man and the values of life. The fact that a baby is to itself the centre of the universe is inevitable and not actually sinful ; it is only wrong because not even the baby is wholly an individual. It is very possible, as the Fathers taught, that " original sin " involves damage to that human nature which we share, but, quite strictly, we should speak not of fallen human nature, but of the human nature of fallen human beings. Hence it should be quite clear what is meant by the assertion that the Word assumed human nature but not " original sin."

But how is this to be conceived? There is hidden in the heart of every man the mystery of his own ego, his own ultimate personality. We are mysteries to ourselves, and much more to others. If I no longer ascribe to the sin of Adam and its transmission through natural generation the tendencies to evil and the prejudices and false judgments that are in me, and if I cannot cast the blame for all my faults and sins upon my environment and my heredity, to what do I ascribe my sins ? To free will. But why do I, being free, choose evil ? Because of past sins which have weakened my will and perverted my judgment ? But there must have been some first original act of will, when I was a child. Being my first sin, it cannot be ascribed to the baleful influence of earlier sins. How came that first sin? I must ascribe it to some twist, some perversion, some defect in my initial personality before ever there was conscious choice or moral sin in me. That, too, is "original sin" – that state which is presupposed by all actual sin. All men are alike here. We cannot deny the guilt of our actual sins, and when we analyse far enough the mystery of our personality, of that *hypostasis*, that ego, which is the secret of our personality, we find that fateful flaw. The *hypostasis*, which is the ultimate concrete *ego* of every man, is a "fallen" personality; every human, as such, is fallen. The classical doctrine of the Person of Christ is that He truly assumed human nature, but that in His case the *hypostasis* of human nature was not a fallen personality, but the eternal Word of God. That is to say, He assumed a human mind, a human body, a human psychological constitution, but the centre of His individual Being was not a fallen human personality, but very God Himself.

The Word made flesh

This is, no doubt, a very difficult conception, but we may pause to note that it is close both to the Christian revelation and to the indications of the Gospels. As regards the revelation, unless we deny "original sin," this doctrine is almost an exact transcription of what we must mean by the Incarnation; it implies that as human nature is the instrument used by us fallen human personalities through which in this world to express our personality, so this human nature is the instrument used by God Himself in that divine self-expression which is our redemption. We see, too, why a human personality cannot be ascribed to our Lord, for a human personality is bound by "original sin." As regards the Gospels, we are compelled to recognize the true and real humanity of our

Lord, but we do not see in Him the traces of "original sin," such as spiritual growth through struggle, defeat, and victory, the gradual attainment of unity and peace, which is the story of the saints. Further, we must see the truth underlying the old adage, *aut deus aut non bonus* – either He was God or not a good man. As man He said, "I thirst," but not as man He said, "I came not to call the righteous but sinners"; "whosoever receiveth you receiveth Me, and whosoever receiveth Me receiveth not Me but Him that sent Me"; "Come unto Me all ye that labour and are heavy laden . . . take My yoke upon you and learn of Me, for I am meek and lowly in heart"; "None knoweth the Father save the Son"; "the Son of Man came . . . to give His life a ransom for many"; "this cup is the New Covenant in My blood." If a man spoke like that he would be by common consent insane; but Christ's healing of the demoniacs was proof enough, if proof were needed, of His sanity. It is important always to bear in mind that the complicated problems of Christology are not due to the mystifications of the theologians, but are set by the Person of Jesus Christ as He is presented to us in the Gospels.

The Two Natures

None the less, there are grave difficulties not easily to be resolved in the classical tradition. God Himself, it is said, without laying aside anything of His Godhead, assumed a human body, a human mind, a human soul. That God should use a human body as His immediate instrument is not, perhaps, a too difficult conception. The gravest difficulties arise when we attempt to conceive the mental and spiritual life of the Incarnate Word. The classical doctrine asserts, for instance, that He had two wills – a divine and a human. This, however, is not so difficult as it sounds to us, for "will" here does not mean what it means to us. There is, as we should say, an impulse, an instinct, an urge, in every living thing to attain to that which it was meant to be – thus the acorn strives to become an oak, a child a man. This urge to fulfilment or completion, to be in fact what it is in idea, is part of our human nature ; it is the same urge or instinct in all men. Therefore the Incarnate Word being made man shared in the human will. There must be conceived to be in God that which is analogous to the human will, but in His case it must be the will, not to become what He is not yet, but to be what He is. The Two Wills doctrine, therefore, follows naturally from the idea of Incarnation.

But the classical doctrine seems to imply that Christ had two minds or two consciousnesses, so that it is said of Him that sometimes He spoke and acted as God, sometimes as man. Thus, as man, He said, " I thirst," as man He ate, but as God he said, " thy sins be forgiven thee," and, as God, rose from the dead. At first sight this seems to us to introduce an element of complete unreality into the Gospel stories, and to involve the supposition of a dual personality in our Lord. But nothing is more certain than that the Fathers asserted with passionate vehemence His single, undivided Personality. In our modern sense of the word " will," as indicating the expression of the whole personality, He had one will.

There is, indeed, no means of escape from unfathomable mystery when we contemplate the Person of our Lord. But possibly two illustrations from normal human experience may offer a little light. As a man the Christian minister eats his meals and takes his rest at night, and as a man he preaches. But his preaching belongs to his prophetic office ; he may signify this by prefacing his sermon with the words, " In the Name of the Father and of the Son and of the Holy Ghost" ; in any case he speaks, with an authority that is not his own, a message which is not his, though he accepts it ; in God's Name he preaches to himself as well as to his congregation. This no more involves a dual personality or dual consciousness than does the experience of Her Majesty, who speaks sometimes as a woman and a mother, sometimes as the Queen. This is an illustration, not a parallel ; but it suggests that it is not nonsense to allege that Christ ate and slept as man, but taught and healed as the Incarnate Word.

But the Fathers often say that as man Christ suffered, not as God, for the Deity must be impassible. Yet for this, too, we may offer a very tentative parallel which may help to give reality to the conception. A man may suffer, and may at the same time contemplate his suffering and bid himself be brave in the bearing of it ; a Christian may be suffering, and yet at the same time, because he is a Christian, enjoy peace and beatitude in spite of, and even through, his suffering. We might speak, in these cases, of different levels of consciousness, but we should not suggest a double or divided personality. Thus when the Fathers said that as man Christ suffered, they did not in any degree deny the undivided Personality of the incarnate Word. What they did deny was that the Word assumed a human personality (that of Jesus the human prophet), for that would have involved a duality of personality.

A greater difficulty underlies the spiritual life of our Lord – His prayers ; His obedience ; His faith. It is not enough to say that here He was acting as our example. This is to make His religious life unreal. We can say, however, that the need for prayer, obedience, and faith, not less than hunger and thirst, belongs to human nature as such. If, therefore, the Word assumed human nature,

He assumed therewith these needs. We obey, and believe in, and pray to, that which is not ourselves. But if we may consider different levels of consciousness in ourselves, such that, for instance, we doubt in our moods what we believe in our hearts, is it to be thought meaningless that He as man obeyed, and believed in, and prayed to, that Being which He knew to be of one nature with Himself?

We are altogether out of our depth here. This assuredly is the sphere of theology and not of dogma. The Incarnation itself is dogma as the transcript of the revelation. But that which is ultimately implied for thought in the Christian "story" is not part of the story itself. Shall we deny, then, that the doctrine that our Lord has two Natures in one Person is a dogma of the faith?

A necessary dogma?

What exactly would our "denial" mean? Strictly it would mean a denial either that He was God or that He was man; but neither of these could be denied without a rejection of the revelation itself. If the denial meant merely a refusal to be committed to all the intensely difficult implications which theologians have attempted to work out, that would be no denial of the Incarnation, but merely the necessary confession that it is mystery insoluble.

If the Incarnation can be better expressed than in the Two Natures doctrine, we may rejoice. But there seems at present no alternative. As we have seen, an Adoptionist Christology will not serve, for there are insuperable philosophical, moral, and religious objections to the view that the Word assumed a human personality. Again, we speak sometimes of Kenotic theories, based on the idea of the "self-emptying" of God; but it is a question whether we can properly call this suggestion in itself a "theory"; it is rather the declaration than the illumination of our darkness. Again, the Ritschlian phrase that Christ has for us " the value of God " has become very popular, but it is not intellectually clear, though it may be spiritually helpful. That which has the value of a thing is presumably that thing itself; if the saying that Christ has for us the value of God does not mean that Christ is God, but rather that He is somehow different, it is precisely this difference which Christology must define. The mere fact, however, that we have no alternative to the Two Natures doctrine does not of itself confirm that doctrine.

Can we say, then, that the Two Natures is a necessary doctrine, and therefore in some sense a dogma? On the one side, it is plain that much of the profound speculation concerning the Person of Christ belongs to the sphere of theology and is not immediately given in the deposit of faith; on the other side, the apprehension both of God and of man in Christ is of the very essence of the revelation. It is, I suppose, theoretically conceivable that human thought should outgrow the category of " nature " and thus cease to treat of " human nature," just as it is conceivable that the physical sciences should outgrow the category of " matter." That is a speculative question. But, so long as we continue to think of " human nature," we shall only be in harmony with the Christian revelation if we say that in Christ are two natures in one Person; but, as with the progress of science, psychology, and philosophy, we come to a clearer understanding of human nature, we may hope to express the Two Natures doctrine in a form more easily intelligible.

I have already indicated that between dogma (in the sense in which the term is here used) and theology there is no absolute line of demarcation; for the term "dogma" is applied not only to the statement of the acts of God, but also to the immediate, necessary implications of these acts for thought. Is the Two Natures doctrine dogma in the sense of immediate necessary implication of the revelation? Yes, in the sense that His being very God and very man necessarily implies, and is at once seen to imply, that He has in one Person both the nature of God and the nature of man. No, in the sense that the revelation cannot immediately be said to imply that the divine Word became the *hypostasis* of human nature. There seems to be no necessary finality about this theory, although we cannot propound a better; and even if the classical doctrine be shown to be logically necessary, it would lack the immediacy of dogma; for the Christian "story" can be told without any reference to "two wills" or "two minds" or "two energies," but it cannot be told without the assertion (in some form of words or other) that God "was made man" – that is, that He assumed our nature without loss of His own.

In the Nicene Creed it stands written: "I believe . . . in one Lord Jesus Christ, the only-begotten Son of God, begotten of His Father before all worlds, God of God, Light of Light, very God of very God, begotten not made, being of one substance with the Father, by whom all things were made: who for us men, and for our salvation, came down from heaven, and was incarnate by the Holy Ghost of the Virgin Mary, and was made man . . ." This is not quite dogma (in our sense) because the Christian "story" can be understood by those who could not understand every phrase of the creed; it is, however, in substance dogma, because it tells the Christian "story," and adds nothing that is not implicit in the story. "And was made man," is the fundamental dogma.

Chapter IX

THE RESURRECTION

I

IS the confession, " He is risen," a dogma of the faith? And, if so, what precisely does it mean? Is the modern Christian required to believe in the empty tomb and in the physical Resurrection of the Lord? Is the Resurrection truly an historical event, or is it, rather, some sort of spiritual event?

The evidence

First we may briefly consider the evidence. The testimony of St. Paul cannot be set on one side. We have letters by him the authenticity of which must be accepted. St. Paul was well acquainted with St. Peter, for, as he himself tells us, he went up to Jerusalem, some time after his conversion, " to learn Cephas' story "; he stayed with him a fortnight, and met St. James, the Lord's brother, at the same time. Writing to the Church in Corinth, later, St. Paul gives a short epitome of the Gospel which he received from those who were Christians before him: " I delivered unto you first of all that which I also received, that Christ . . . died . . . and that He was buried, and that He rose again the third day according to the Scriptures: and that He was seen of Cephas, then of the twelve: after that, He was seen of above five hundred brethren at once; of whom the greater part remain unto this present, but some are fallen asleep. After that, He was seen of James; then of all the apostles." Finally St. Paul adds that he himself saw Him.

From this it may with certainty be concluded that more than five hundred persons, including St. Paul himself, our authority, and at least two others known to him personally, were convinced that they had actually seen the Lord after His death. Either they saw Him or, at least, they thought they saw Him. That much is clear and indubitable.

It is open to the incredulous to say that these witnesses suffered from an hallucination, and, even if it be impossible to give any satisfactory account of the origin of this hallucination, our evidence will not convince the sceptic that Christ really triumphed over death. It will be noticed, too, that St. Paul apparently dates the Resurrection not by the evidence of the empty tomb on Easter Sunday, but by some obscure reference to Scripture.

What, then, of the empty tomb? The Christian tradition, which rests upon the evidence of the Gospels, is that the dead body of the Lord was "changed" or glorified, that He, in His thus glorified body, left the tomb in which He had been laid; hence the tomb was found empty by the women when they came to anoint His body on the morning of Easter Sunday.

We may put on one side the objection of those who say that such a miracle is inconceivable. As Christians we are considering the alleged Resurrection of the Incarnate Word, of One who was very God as well as very man. If we believe in the Incarnation, the addition of the belief in His "physical" Resurrection will not add a noticeable burden to faith. But, admitted that the "physical" Resurrection is not incredible, we still must ask, did it really happen? Is the evidence cogent to the mind of faith?

There can be no doubt that our evidence is confused or

puzzling. There is the apparent lack of harmony between the various narratives of the Resurrection appearances. There is the unexplained failure of the first three Gospels to narrate the appearance of the Lord to St. Peter. The Fourth Gospel, indeed, tells of this appearance, but locates it in Galilee, and there is other evidence, too, that the Lord's appearances were in Galilee. Then there is the silence of St. Paul about the empty tomb. It is not surprising that serious and not unbelieving scholars have argued that amid such obscurity it is wisest to suppose that St. Paul's evidence far outweighs the much later tradition of the Gospels, that such stories as do not fit in with St. Paul's account are to be suspected as pious legends, and that it is precisely the Holy Sepulchre narratives which are most open to suspicion. On the other side, it is argued that from the first the Christians proclaimed the Resurrection, that had the tomb not been empty the Jews would have been quick to make use of so formidable a weapon of argument, and that St. Paul must have believed in the empty tomb, since he could not have taught that our bodies will be "changed" into the likeness of Christ's Resurrection body, unless he already believed that the Lord's body had been "glorified."

This is a very brief summary of a most intricate and perplexing question. The right conclusion from it is that from a purely literary or historic point of approach no certain conclusion can be drawn; for even if we could prove by the canons of scientific historical criticism that the tomb was empty on Easter Sunday, we could not prove by any such method that the Lord's body had been changed and glorified. If, therefore, there is proof of the "physical" Resurrection (to use the current term), it must be a dogmatic proof – that is, it must be shown that the " change " and glorification of the Lord's body and its escape from the tomb are an integral part of the Christian " story." Can this be shown?

II

The Christian " story " is that God's Son came down from heaven, lived and died on earth, and rose again, returning whence He came. It will not be suggested that the " story " can be told without these elements. But is the ultimate fate of the Lord's " flesh," in the literal sense of the term, an integral part of the story?

" Body " distinguished from " flesh "

We must note a difference in St. Paul's usage between "flesh" and "body." St. Paul asserts that our " bodies " shall be " changed "; he also asserts that " flesh and blood " shall not inherit the Kingdom. By " body " he means not something physical, but rather a principle of identity. For instance, I bear in my body a scar made by a surgeon's knife some thirty years and more ago. I have been told that during this thirty years all the physical particles of my body have changed, so that physically nothing remains of that flesh which the surgeon cut; but the scar remains. There is a non-physical principle of identity in the human body (or, to take another example, in a river) which makes it permanently the same body (or river) though it be physically in a state of constant flux. St. Paul tells us that the body, which is our principle of identity, and which now is suited to our earthly environment, shall one day be suited to our heavenly environment. This, it is said, is the true doctrine of the resurrection of the body; it has nothing whatever to do with flesh and blood, which are purely physical. So in the case of our Lord it would not be necessary to suppose that any change took place in His physical frame, His flesh and blood. We must for the moment leave the matter at this point; for not till we have considered more fully what is meant by the Resurrection faith can we determine whether or not a physical change in the body is implied in it.

The Resurrection appearances

We turn, then, to the Resurrection appearances of Christ. Did the disciples see Him or only think they saw Him? First, we are not required to suppose that the disciples saw that which, to put it crudely, a camera could photograph, for a camera can photograph only that which is material. It may be replied that we are told elsewhere that the Lord ate with His disciples after He suffered, and must therefore have had a material body. We shall be wise, however, to start from the contemporary evidence of St. Paul, and if, as is clear, he declares that Christ's body was "spiritual" – that is, not material or "fleshly" after the Resurrection – we shall do well either to question this later tradition of the Gospel or interpret it, if we can, in harmony with St. Paul's teaching. We should not maintain, then, that the disciples saw a material body.

Were they the victims, then, of an hallucination? We must draw a clear distinction between what I will call hallucination and vision. We have a case of hallucination, when, as for instance in delirium, we see, or seem to see, things although they are not there. We have vision when we see, or seem to see, things which are there, although they are not normally visible, being spiritual. We may say, then, that the disciples saw the Lord, not because for certain obscure psychological reasons they were subject to self-deception supposing the Lord to be there when in fact He was far away, but rather because they were so vividly and suddenly aware of His actual and indubitable living Presence with them, that this spiritual fact was objectified in the form of a vision.

This may, or may not, be the best way to understand the appearances ; what is of more importance is that the Resurrection faith does not rest either upon the empty tomb or upon " appearances." As Professor Karl Adam points out, the women finding the tomb empty may merely be dismayed – " they have taken away my Lord, and I know not where they have laid Him " – and the disciples seeing the Lord may think it is a ghost and be merely frightened. Christ Himself said : " If they believe not Moses and the prophets, they will not believe though one rise from the dead." Neither the empty tomb nor the appearances by themselves account for the Resurrection faith, though they give it support and confirmation.

The Resurrection faith

What, then, is the Resurrection faith ? The Apostles' Creed runs : " was crucified, dead, and buried, He descended into hell ; the third day He rose again from the dead. He ascended into heaven, and sitteth on the right hand of God the Father almighty . . ." We have here a number of statements – His death, His Resurrection, His descent into hell, His Ascension, His session at the right hand of God. In fact, we have a " story " telling of the victorious return of Him who at the first Christmas came down to earth " in the form of a servant." If the Incarnation is one " mighty act " of God, the Resurrection with the Ascension is another. We shall best grasp the Resurrection faith by taking all these elements in the story together.

In the earlier chapter on the Idea of Revelation I urged

that our Lord came, not primarily to give us imperishable maxims of moral and spiritual truth, but " to destroy the works of the devil, and to make us sons of God and heirs of eternal life," and that His life is to be interpreted as a conflict with the powers of darkness and a bringing of the Kingdom. It is from this standpoint alone that we can understand the Resurrection faith. The Resurrection is not survival ; it is victory.

We speak to-day of the " forces " of darkness, of sin, of evil. In the same sort of way St. Paul and those of his day could speak of Sin and Death as quasi-personified demonic forces, or our Lord could speak of Satan and Beelzebub. Let me, then, retell the story keeping to the imagery of Scripture and the creeds, and, for the moment, giving no thought to the retranslation of this faith into modern terms.

The Son of God was manifested to destroy the works of the devil and make us sons of God and heirs of eternal life. For this end He took our nature upon Him and became man. The narrative of the Temptation at the beginning of His ministry we may call His first brush with the enemy. His public ministry, with its mighty words and mighty works, was His bringing of the Kingdom, His driving out of Satan " by the finger of God." He appeared at first to be succeeding : " Behold, I saw Satan as lightning fall from heaven " ; the Strong Man was bound. But in the end, as it seemed, the enemy was too much for Him. He had to flee from Galilee ; He went up to Jerusalem, and for a few days His *coup d'état* seemed to succeed ; for He taught in the Temple, none being able to prevent Him ; but He was tripped upon a political charge ; His popularity deserted Him ; at last even His disciples left Him and fled ; He was hurriedly tried and executed ;

and a great sigh of relief went up from all His enemies ; He was caught and silenced at last. Dead, he descended, like all the shades, to " hell " – not the place of torment, but the dim region of the departed ; and, when he entered, the gates clanged after Him, and Death and Sin had triumphed. He descended into hell, a shade, as it seemed, among the shades. But, if the gate clanged fast behind Him, it was impossible that He should be holden of it. As once Samson had come out from Gaza carrying the brazen gates upon his shoulders, so the " most glorious Lord of life " came up out of hell, having broken down its gates, and returned, bringing His saints with Him ; for forty days He appeared to His disciples and assured them of His victory ; thence, having broken the power of the enemy and thrown open the gates of everlasting life to all believers, He ascended to heaven and took His seat on the throne of the Universe. His reign already has begun, and of His Kingdom there shall be no end.

That is the story. Let it be admitted from the first that it is largely mythological in form. It cannot be literally true in any scientific or purely historical sense. But, as we have seen, it is only in the language of a story that the mighty acts of God can be expressed.

This story crosses history at two points. When the Lord descended into hell, as do all the departed, His body, of course, remained within the tomb. When He returned triumphant from death, He appeared to His disciples. What is the significance of all the rest ? Does it in any degree depend upon a cosmology which would put the abode of the shades below the earth and heaven in the sky ?

A common modern reconstruction would be along these lines : " We believe that Christ was crucified and buried.

His body, of course, remained in the grave, and suffered corruption as must ours; but He himself was not destroyed by death; not merely does His work go forward and His memory prove a powerful influence amongst mankind, but His spirit is with us still to help and console and save. Because we believe this, we believe all that is essential in the Easter message."

But it can hardly be thought that this is a representation of the "story" of the Resurrection, the descent into hell, the Ascension and the Session at the right hand. It is asserted, indeed, that Christ is still in some sense alive; but the assumption is that for all of us death is only the destruction of the body; thus what was to have been the triumphal doctrine of the Resurrection is contorted into the view that Christ is as dead as in the nature of the case it is possible for any one to be. The denial of the supernatural and miraculous is the plain denial of "the story." The fact that this reconstruction can be set forth in simple and straightforward terms is itself an indication that no "act of God" is being described. Nothing is more certain, however, about the Resurrection faith of the disciples than that they saw in Christ's rising the signal act of God in the defeat of the enemy and the vindication of His Son.

The Resurrection faith is not in any true way represented by the view that, though Christ's body was destroyed, His soul is immortal, and that His spirit is a potent influence upon us. The Resurrection is not survival but victory.

Victory over what? Luther would answer, at once, "Over sin and death, the devil, and the law," but this reply is still obscure to us. We may say more simply that the Resurrection was God's "mighty act" in the vindication of His Son. It is much more than the familiar truth that martyrs do not die in vain, and that their influence lives on. " John Brown's body," we sing, " lies a-mouldering in the grave, but his soul goes marching on." This is not resurrection, but immortality at most. The return of Lazarus, again, from his three days' sojourn in the grave is the resuscitation of a corpse, not resurrection. The supernatural Resurrection is, as we shall see, not to be sundered from the supernatural sending of the Holy Ghost.

In the period of the Old Testament the Lord, the God of Israel, had from time to time " laid bare His mighty arm " in the deliverance of His people ; but for centuries the story of Israel had rather been an ever more desperate waiting for a Kingdom that never came. " How long, O Lord, how long ? " ; " Thou art a God that hidest Thyself " ; " Clouds and darkness are round about Him." At last had come One who had seemed to promise more than a fulfilment of all men's highest dreams ; He had declared the immeasurable love and compassion of God, who has numbered all the hairs of our head, who sends His sun and His rain upon just and unjust, thankful and thankless, apart from whose care not a sparrow falls to the ground ; He had bidden men cast all their care on God, taking no thought for the morrow, knowing well that their heavenly Father, who clothes the lilies and feeds the ravens, will take good care of His children. At first this teaching had seemed, as we say, to " work " ; the sick had been healed, and Satan driven back. The Teacher Himself was the test case of His teaching ; if ever there was a child of God it was He ; if ever there was one wholly obedient, wholly dedicated, wholly faithful, it was He. If this teaching about God were true, God must protect His Son. And God had let Him die – in pain and ignominy and desertion, with every attendant circumstance of horror. Life had been too much for theory, grim facts for such a pleasant sentimentalism. The Cross seemed to mark the denial of all the gracious teaching about the love and Providence of God; it was more than a bitter question-mark against the sky; it showed that ours is a God-forsaken world; it is the devil's world; it is the world in which the Son of Man, the bravest, the gentlest, the most selfless and compassionate that ever lived, must suffer crucifixion.

If this be the end of the story, how did the disciples ever come to declare that He was risen? They might believe in the general resurrection at the Last Day, but, as Jews, they had no antecedent expectation of a private prior resurrection for individuals. Whence, then, this colossal self-deception and public imposture? Neither the empty tomb nor the appearances account for it; the appearances themselves must be accounted for, if they were but hallucination. Or did the disciples comfort themselves with the sober conviction that, after all, their Master might be dead, but His spirit would live on; they must let Him influence their lives, and carry on His work as best they could; and thus, when every hope had been shattered, their Master slain, and His teaching about God proved moonshine, they went forth over the Roman Empire conquering and to conquer? The way of unbelievers is hard indeed!

The Cross seemed the end, the final discomfiture, of the teaching of the Lord. But it was not primarily as Teacher that He came. He declared the advent of the Kingdom; He brought the Kingdom; from first to last He bade men know that God's arm was outstretched, that He would do such a mighty work of redemption as should be comparable only to the morning of Creation ; a new era had dawned ; the Messianic age was come. If the Cross ends the story, Christ was the great Deceiver because He was the great Deceived. He proclaimed and anticipated miracle ; if all that happened was that His influence has lived on, then He was indeed deceived and our faith is vain ; how foolish we should be to trust God, when He, who taught us, trusted God, and God abandoned Him !

" What we are dealing with," says Dr. Karl Adam, " is not the raising up of a mere man, but the Resurrection of the Christ, not the mere flaming up of an extinct natural life, but the creative breaking through of that divine life, which Jesus from the very beginning knew to be His own in the perishable frame of His mortal body, and which now on the third day after His death, reuniting soul and body, clothed and glorified His whole human nature with the majesty of God." The attempt to explain away the Resurrection as if it were not miracle is a repudiation, not merely of the Resurrection narratives in the Gospels, but of the Gospels as a whole. Let it be admitted, for the sake of argument, that the precise predictions of the Resurrection ascribed to our Lord in the Gospels may be coloured after the event ; none the less, He began His ministry by the proclamation of the coming miraculous intervention of God ; He proved His message by His miracles and His words of power ; He declared that according to the purpose of God the Son of Man must suffer many things ; on His last night on earth He bade His disciples look forward to the fellowship of the Kingdom which He would share with them beyond His death. God's vindication of Him was the Resurrection and the Church, for Easter and Pentecost are indissolubly bound together.

III

The "physical" Resurrection

Are the empty tomb and the "physical" Resurrection integral and necessary elements in this miracle and in this faith? As regards the "empty tomb," we cannot say that its emptiness on Easter Sunday can be proved by history – that would be too much to demand of the historian; we can say, however, that it is well attested, and that it can only be contradicted on the basis of very uncertain theories. It is not the emptiness of the tomb in itself, but the reason for that emptiness that is of significance for Christian doctrine. Was it empty because on the third day after His death Christ's soul rejoined His body and with it issued in glory from the tomb? This is the orthodox Christian doctrine. Is it a necessary part of the "story"? The question is not, Did a miracle happen? – for miracle in the sense of a mighty act of God is of the essence of the Resurrection faith – but, Is this particular "physical" miracle involved? I think the answer is that the "story" can be told without this element. The chief ground for this answer is that there is some evidence that the "story" has actually been told in the earliest days without this element.

Thus, St. Paul, as we have seen, apparently dates the Resurrection "on the third day," not from the discovery of the women at the tomb, but from some prophecy in the Old Testament. Again, there is the strange comparison of Christ's sojourn in the tomb with Jonah's sojourn in the whale for "three days and three nights" – a very much longer period than from Good Friday afternoon till early on Easter Sunday. Once more, there is the story in the Gospels that on the night of the Crucifixion the saints came out of their graves and walked in the streets of Jerusalem. This presupposes that the gates of " hell " have been thrown open, and seems, therefore, to be implicitly inconsistent with the view that Christ remained in " hell " till the third day. This is confirmed by the custom of the Asian Church in the early centuries ; for it celebrated the Crucifixion and the Resurrection on the same day. All this does not disprove the accepted tradition of the Church that our Lord broke from the tomb on Easter Sunday, but it at least suggests that the dating of the Resurrection " on the third day " is not essential to the story.

There is a further consideration. The classical tradition implies, and, indeed, actually states, that from Good Friday evening till early on Easter Sunday the Lord's soul abode in the place of the shades and then rejoined His body. Whatever may have been the interpretation of this in the Early Church, we cannot take the " descent into hell " literally. It is, as we shall see, a spiritual event, but it is not an historical event ; for history deals only with this life and this world. Moreover, the rejoining of soul and body, not in the sense of a reanimation of a dead person, but involving also a " glorification " of the body, cannot at first sight be said to be necessarily implied in the Incarnation itself, and therefore to be a dogma.

On the other hand, the recognition of the first day of the week as the day of the Resurrection goes back to the earliest days ; it was part of that tradition which St. Paul received from those who were Christians before him – that is, we may claim for it the authority or consent of St. Peter and St. James. It is extraordinarily difficult by the canons of history to set aside such evidence. But still we are forced back on the question, Does this involve the "physical" Resurrection? If the tomb was empty on Easter Sunday, and we deny the "physical" Resurrection, we should have to say that the Lord's body had been stolen and hidden – unless, indeed, the women went in error to the wrong grave. But we are asking, not what is the most probable or reasonable answer, but whether the "physical" Resurrection is a dogma. It is only a dogma if it can be shown to be essential to the redeeming work of Christ; that is the matter to be discussed in the next chapter. We may, however, here anticipate our conclusion by saying that both with regard to the Virgin Birth and the Resurrection, regarded as "physiological" facts, we are not, in the present state of our knowledge and understanding, in a position to state categorically that the Christian "story" cannot be told without these elements. If we believe in the Incarnate Word, there may seem nothing strange in these beliefs, but it is another matter to assert that they are dogmas.

The Resurrection stands for the mighty act of God in the vindication of His Son and for His victory over sin and death. This leads direct to the subject of the next chapter, which is the Atonement or redeeming work of Christ. Since the Resurrection is Victory, it can only be expressed by active verbs and in the form of narrative; it is action, not idea; dogma, not theology. The Resurrection – and that, too, not in the sense of survival or immortality, but in the sense of victory – is one of those elements without which the Christian "story" cannot be told. It is, therefore, dogma in the strictest sense.

"He descended into hell"

Likewise the descent into hell is dogma, though it is not so much as mentioned in the Nicene Creed. By this is not meant that the clause can be taken literally, or that the spiritual facts which it represents cannot be put in any other terms, but that it stands for an essential moment in the Christian "story." Christ, the incarnate Word, had wrought our salvation for us who by grace believe in Him; but does His salvation extend only to His contemporaries and His successors? What of the saints who "all died in faith not having seen the promises, but having greeted them afar off"? They also must be heirs of the Kingdom. This sublime and necessary truth is here set forth in the form that the Lord went down to Sheol and set free the spirits that there waited for His coming.

But we may surely go a step further. Millions have lived and died without ever hearing the Saviour's Name. It has often been the hard doctrine of the Church that all these must be consigned to everlasting torment because of their (guiltless) unbelief. The basis of this doctrine has been certain texts of Scripture which do not inevitably bear this construction. Such a view can hardly be a dogma, since it does not spring from, nor even conform to, the revelation of God in Christ as One who loves to the uttermost, as the Shepherd who goes out after the one lost sheep "till He find." The doctrine of the Descent into Hell and "the harrowing of hell" stands for the victorious act of Christ in vanquishing the power of death; it declares, not, indeed, that all men shall be saved, but that the Gospel extends not only to the Church, but to the great multitude of the human family.

But may we call this a dogma? Yes, for it tells of the act of God and is implicitly bound up with the Christian "story." For the Christian "story" is that, because man was lost in wretchedness and woe, the divine Redeemer came to save not merely those who might be fortunate enough to hear His Name and put their trust in Him, but all mankind. This is the doctrine of the salvability, but not of the inevitable or automatic salvation, of all men ; it is the universal moment in the Gospel. True, we may tell the " story " without any reference to the descent to the shades below – and possibly, in these unpoetical days, it is better so to tell it ; but we cannot tell it without that which the " descent " implies if we are to declare the essential element in the Gospel that Jesus Christ is the Saviour of the world.

The Ascension

Is the Ascension an historical event ? We read that from the Mount of Olives the disciples saw their Master rise heavenwards till a cloud hid Him from their eyes. It is, I think, idle to speculate upon the accuracy of this account, for two reasons : first, we do not believe that heaven is a geographical district directly above Palestine ; thus the Lord's Ascension from the Mount of Olives could be taken only as the sign of His return to heaven, not as the return itself ; second, though the experiences of the disciples might be a proper study for historical or psychological enquiry, the historian as such would not discuss this narrative. The Ascension is dogma, however, because it is of the essence of the " story." The Son of God came down to earth from heaven, and, having accomplished His task, He returned whence He came. It is the Conqueror's triumphal entry into the eternal City.

Who is this that comes from Edom,
All His raiment stained with blood ;
To the captive speaking freedom,
Bringing and bestowing good ;
Glorious in the garb He wears,
Glorious in the spoil He bears ?

'Tis the Saviour, now victorious,
Travelling onward in His might;
'Tis the Saviour, O how glorious
To his people is the sight!
Satan conquer'd and the grave,
Jesus now is strong to save.

This the Saviour hath effected
By His mighty arm alone;
See the throne, for Him erected,
'Tis an everlasting throne;
'Tis the great reward He gains,
Glorious fruit of all His pains.

What but this is the end of the story? The narratives of the Garden of Eden are not prosaic history, but in the beginning, as they declare, the enemy of souls deceived mankind; through the long centuries Sin and Ignorance and Fear and Death held men in thrall. Then in the appointed hour the Great Deliverer came; dying, he slew death, and ransomed the captive children of earth. Henceforward He shall reign for ever, and of His Kingdom there shall be no end.

But not yet do we see all things subject to Him; not yet is the consummation; therefore it still remains to speak of the Church as well as of the work of Christ in reconciliation.

Chapter X

THE ATONEMENT

IT has been customary in certain circles to contrast the Gospel of the Kingdom with the Gospel of the Cross, the " Gospel of Jesus " with the " Gospel about Jesus," and to see in St. Paul the founder of ecclesiastical Christianity, the theologian-evangelist who diverted Christianity from the simplicities of Galilee to the subtleties of metaphysical speculation.

It is possible that St. Paul was the first to " glory in " the Cross and to regard the Cross as a positive centre of his faith rather than as the inevitable prelude to the Resurrection. But that " Christ died for our sins according to the Scriptures " was, as he explicitly tells us, part of the tradition of the Church which he received when he became a Christian. That Christ died for our sins is, indeed, a dogma of the faith, because the Christian " story " cannot be told without it. But, whereas in the case of the Trinity and the Incarnation we have received a classical doctrine which we may say has been received by the Church for sixteen hundred years and more as the expression of its faith, we have no such œcumenical doctrine of the Atonement.

Three types of doctrine

We have, rather, three types of doctrine, one which, laying the great stress on the Incarnation, declares that we are saved because the Word took human nature upon Him and thus united it with God; the second which, emphasizing the death of Christ, declares that it is by

" His precious blood " that we are saved ; and the third which, putting the accent upon the life and teaching of Christ (with His death as the final expression of His life and teaching), declares that Christ saves us by winning our hearts.

But this brief summary needs much qualification ; indeed, it might not unfairly be represented that the difference between these expressions is, or may be, a matter rather of form than substance. Thus, for instance, St. John of Damascus, who, in his philosophical theology, seems to prove our redemption by the fact of the Incarnation, shows his heart when in language that is either lyrical or mythological he speaks about the Cross ; nor may we forget his assumption that we appropriate the fruits of the Incarnation in the sacraments which are inseparably connected with the Cross. Or, again, St. Anselm, who is popularly taken to be sponsor for the view that it is the death of Christ which ransoms us, sets as the title of his treatise the question, " Why was the Incarnation necessary ? "—*Cur Deus homo ?* Finally, the third view may sometimes be put in the form that it was the very purpose of the Incarnation and of the death of Christ to awaken us to truth and quicken us to righteousness. In the case of the Atonement, where there is no one classical theology, it should be easier than in the case of the Trinity and the Incarnation to distinguish form from substance. Our concern is with the meaning, the substance, and the implications of the dogma that Christ died for our sins.

I

Let me set forth a modern " restatement " of the doctrine which, implicitly or explicitly, is widely held :

A modern "restatement"

"It is absurd to suggest that Christ died nearly two thousand years ago for the sins I have committed in my lifetime, nor is it credible that the death of Christ made possible God's forgiveness of my sins; for God, as Christ taught, is willing to accept the penitent and to run to meet him, if only he be penitent and turn his face towards his Father's house. Therefore the death of Christ can only affect my sins by affecting my heart. But I accept the doctrine that Christ died for my sins, because it was sins like mine which brought Him to His death, and, furthermore, in that death He reveals to me the love and forgiveness of God, and so touches my heart that I lose my relish for sin and thus am delivered from it. I say, then, that Christ died for my sins chiefly because by His death He reveals and brings home to me the love of God."

This "restatement" avoids the objections which can legitimately be laid against the older theologies of the Atonement, but it does not go deep enough to be really a restatement of that religious intuition which gave to the older views their passion and their power. I shall suggest that it is inadequate chiefly on three grounds: first, that it does not treat seriously enough of sin and guilt and shame; second, that it is too purely individual and subjective to represent that victory of Christ which we apprehend in the Resurrection and that "finished work" of Christ which is represented in our baptism; third, that, in general, it is unrelated to that which we have seen to be the fundamental Christian dogma – the Incarnation; it offers us the influence of the ideal man for the Passion of the Incarnate Word; if this were the substance of the Christian dogma, St. Anselm might have called his book, not *Cur Deus homo?* but *Num Deus homo?* – not, "Why was the Incarnation necessary?" but, "Surely the Incarnation was not necessary?"

If in Jesus Christ we have apprehended God Himself made man for our redemption, then in the Cross, as Professor Karl Adam says, "we are not merely fronted by the heroic act of a holy person obedient unto death to the heavenly Father, but by the death of a man who is God, by the death of our Lord, by the death of one who is the judge of the world. It is an event so dreadful, so past all conception, that the sun pales in the heavens, the earth quakes, and the veil of the temple is rent from top to bottom. Something cosmic is happening here, a world catastrophe. The God-Man is dying. We know very well that God in Himself cannot die. But it is not God, as such, who is dying: it is a man substantially united to the Word of God, a man who *is* God." To him who believes in the Incarnation, or lies under any great conviction of sin, this modern reconstruction seems a very superficial treatment of an overwhelming mystery.

If the Christian "experience" is simply the experience of forgiveness through Christ, and if this modern reconstruction gives an adequate account of that experience, shall we not very properly conclude that the Virgin Birth and the Resurrection, the Trinity and the Incarnation are an unnecessary and incredible addition to "the simple Gospel" – that, in fact, we can have Christianity without its "story," a Christianity free of the mythological and the supernatural? This is the ultimate issue between the "radicals" and "catholics."

II

We have to consider whether the death of our Lord was merely a contingent necessity or also an absolute necessity

"The Son of Man must *suffer"*

– that is to say, whether He was crucified because under the political, social, and religious conditions of His time the tragedy was bound to happen, or was His death necessary for some theological reason as that only by "His blood" can we be saved; is the Cross absolutely necessary for our forgiveness and our salvation?

The scientific historian, as such, who would tell the life of Christ would indicate the state of religious and political parties, the temper of the times, the novelty or danger suspected in the teaching of Christ, and thus show how inevitable it was that, taking the line He did, He should be rejected and be crucified. The historian's narrative might be true, yet it must be very incomplete; for the Christian apprehends in Christ not only a man of His time, but the eternal Word incarnate. The historian, as such, cannot reckon with the Crucifixion of the Son of God; so, too, this modern reconstruction is not based on the evidence of the Gospels, but on psychological considerations which are almost unrelated to the stern objectivity of the Gospels and the teaching of our Lord.

It is not given to us to fathom the innermost thoughts of the Incarnate Word, but we are not left without evidence as to the Cross in the mind of Christ. "The Son of Man," He said, "must suffer many things." Why? Because love must always suffer in a wicked world? True as that may be, it is not His meaning; for such sayings as this are usually, if not always, associated with His journey to Jerusalem. Why *must* the Son of Man suffer? Why *must* He go up to Jerusalem? The necessity was inward and not outward. Humanly speaking, we may say that He might quite well have retired into obscurity, or, being unable to continue His ministry in Palestine, He might have wandered about the world like the Stoic preachers of his time; He might have made His appeal to Athens, where some new thing was always gladly heard, or have sought in liberal Alexandria a more favourable hearing from His fellow-countrymen. The necessity laid upon Him was that of His mission, not of His environment. "The Son of Man came," He said, "to give His life a ransom for many." We may not safely build a theology upon a metaphor; but what is that misery and bondage of men from which, that they be delivered, the Son of Man, God's representative, must die?

Six hundred years before, the prophet Jeremiah, seeing the hopeless and helpless condition of the world, the more desperate for the obdurate blindness of the chosen people and their unwillingness and inability to keep the covenant of righteousness which God had made with their fathers in the beginning, declared in faith that, because God's purposes could not fail, He would make a new covenant with His people, writing His law upon their hearts. Such a new covenant would be not only sheer grace, but sheer miracle. The prophet's word remained a hope and a promise, but how could it be fulfilled without despite to God's moral order with its unalterable principle that no righteousness is of worth unless it be also free? Only a miracle can make man righteous, and righteousness cannot be imposed by miracle; the impasse seems complete.

Our Lord came declaring that God's miracle is at hand. He brought the Kingdom near; but, if the few heard Him gladly, the world would have none of it. The new covenant could not be imposed by divine *fiat* from without. How should it be freely accepted and the world be saved? "This cup is the new covenant *in my blood*": "I, *if I be lifted up*, will draw all men unto Me." The problem of the Atonement is not a mystery introduced unnecessarily into the simplicities of the Christian faith by theologians; it is set by the Gospels themselves and the sayings and actions of our Lord. The mystery of His death is that it is He Who had to die, and that according to His thought, no less than according to traditional theology, His death is necessary for our redemption. Calvary is more than the counterpart in time of the eternal love of God; it is God Himself in His redeeming Act. God is Love – that, indeed, is much, but "In My last hour I thought of thee, drops of My blood I shed for thee," that is the Gospel. It is not merely the temporal reflection of the eternal; it is the Action and Passion of God in time.

I should not wish even to appear to write disparagingly as if it were a little thing that One should in history have shown complete obedience to God and complete trust in Him, and should so have loved His people "unto the end" that not betrayal nor rejection nor scorn nor mortal weakness and agony could change His heart of love to them, and thus reassure us that there must be at the heart of the universe a love not less than this; but in the end this would mean that we are convinced of God's goodness not by the mighty act of God Himself, but by an incomparably good man. This would be untrue alike to the Gospels, to the Christian apprehension that in Christ we meet with very God come for our salvation, and to that deep certainty that the repentance of those who do repent is not adequate to a theodicy, for it is less than is needed for the salvation of the human race and the wiping out of sin.

III

We come back to St. Anselm's phrase, "*Nondum considerasti quanti ponderis sit peccatum*" – "Not yet hast thou considered the gravity of sin"; not yet, we

Repentance and forgiveness

may add, hast thou considered the gravity of forgiveness. It is not a hard thing, when a man has made havoc of his home and in the end has been sent to prison, for the king, if it seem wise to him, to utter a royal pardon. Forgiveness of that kind costs little. It is another thing for the offender's wife and children to forgive. Only the wronged person can truly pardon. No doubt God is infinitely willing to forgive and to receive the penitent and to throw open to him the gates of home, but how can God forgive if He have not suffered? The king, because by wrongdoing he is offended in his dignity, not in his person, must be concerned with justice, and his " pardon " is but a remission of some penalty. There are many who think of God as such a king; He is merciful and kind, they say; He is ever willing to receive the penitent; He will remit the penalty. But this is not the forgiveness of a Father, nor does this meet the deepest need. How shall a man enter the heavenly home and be at peace, if he cannot forgive himself? To be allowed to pay the penalty of his misdeeds and thus to expiate them, to pay his debts and thus be quit of them, no matter how hard the way and how long the time, would be peace and satisfaction. But how shall any man be in heaven, when through the ruin his folly and sin have brought on others, he carries hell about with him?

Which way I fly is hell: myself am hell.

Repentance cannot undo the tragic, bitter past. We have a saying that if a man does so-and-so "there will be the devil to pay"; this is not very different from the old theological principle that a ransom must be paid to the devil. The phrase may be very inexact, but it represents the stern realities of the moral order.

It is a curious superficiality that, since God loves, therefore if only man would repent "everything in the garden would be lovely." When a child is naughty and is sorry, forgiveness follows and the incident is closed. There is in religion the counterpart of this; but sin, as we have seen, is not only the naughtinesses we commit.

A spotless child sleeps on the flowering moss –
'Tis well for him; but when a sinful man
Envying such slumber may desire to put
His guilt away shall he return at once
To rest by lying there? Our sires knew well
(Spite of the grave discoveries of their sons)
The fitting course for such: dank cells, dim lamps,
A stone floor one may writhe on like a worm,
No mossy pillow blue with violets!

No repentance of ours, no tears, no penances, no holocausts, no prayers can undo that which once is done. Saul may repent, but he cannot bring back Stephen from the grave. And even penitence is quite beyond us; our sorrow is so shallow, so transient, so imperfect. And should we truly repent of certain wrongs, still and ever we are compassed about with sin; we neither love God with all our hearts nor our neighbour as ourselves; self and pride creep into the holiest places; the more we advance, the further from the perfect good we seem to be; there is no action, no thought, no desire in us that is not tainted with self and sin; to the grave we carry with us this body of death, this corruption of the spirit, this rebellion against God. Our whole life is sin. "Behold I was shapen in iniquity and in sin did my mother conceive me. . . . And Thou requirest truth in the inward parts. . . . O wretched man that I am, who shall deliver me? . . . I thank God through Jesus Christ."

For lo! between our sins and their reward
We set the Passion of Thy Son our Lord.

Of this mystery we have no satisfactory theory to offer; but the Gospel alone plumbs the depths of our need when it declares that God Himself in the Person of His Son entered into human history, and that our sins and sorrows, our shame and our curse, were borne by Him. As Hooker says, let it be accounted folly or madness, this the Scripture declares and this we believe – that man has sinned and God has suffered, that "Him who knew no sin God made to be sin for us, that we might be the righteousness of God in Him." *Ecce Agnus Dei, ecce qui tollit peccata mundi.*

IV

The Second Adam

Redemption must be effected in the individual, but that is not enough; for we are never merely individuals, but members also of society, of the human race. It is this realization that God must deal with the whole situation, and not merely with individuals, that underlies the classic conception that Christ redeems us by taking our human nature upon Him in the Incarnation. This notion should be more intelligible to us to-day, when alike in politics and economics the old individualism is no more asserted.

We distinguish between actual, voluntary, deliberate sin and that "original sin" in which we are all involved. It is in the first Adam that we are sinners – in the solidarity of the human race; it is in the second Adam that we are redeemed – in the solidarity of a redeemed humanity. This was set forth in the theology of the early Fathers in a form that has repelled modern readers of textbooks because they have understood it in a physical or material sense. In taking our nature upon Him, said the Fathers, Christ linked all humanity with God. Their thought may be illustrated from the human body. That human nature which exists nowhere by itself but is possessed by all men is like the life of the individual, which, being " physical " but not material, has no existence by itself, but is possessed by every part of a man's living body. Brains and hands and feet share the same life; that life, moreover, is not something divisible, such that, if the hand be cut off, there is less life. The life is possessed wholly by every part of the body, for each part lives. If into some part of a body all diseased there should be introduced an element of health, the whole body would not at once be healed; but the new healthy element in that one part of the body would be available for all the rest; the body would be no longer wholly diseased, and in the end the healthy element might drive out all disease. The crucial moment, therefore, in the healing of the body would be the introduction of the new and healthy element. The medical profession might put the matter differently, but an analogy offered as an illustration, not a proof, may serve its purpose. Human nature, which we all possess, as each part of the body possesses the body's life, is, according to the Fathers, intrinsically good but actually " fallen " or diseased. In Adam all men must sin and all must die. But when the Word became incarnate, taking our nature upon Him, He not merely united Himself with our nature, but therein He also united human nature with Divinity. This is the transcript of the declaration in the Gospels that the Kingdom is at hand and that the powers of the age to come are already at work in this present age. Humanity is like the diseased body into which there has been introduced at one point a new and healthy element which will ultimately heal the whole. The appropriation of this new divine element is through faith and through the sacraments.

We need not deny that such a mode of expression may harden into a mechanical or almost automatic conception of salvation, and it is desirable that we seek a form of expression that is more personal; but the old form of the doctrine covers a truth which is of the essence of the matter.

We might put it in this way: each man is an individual, but he is not merely an individual; he is also a member of a family and of society. As a schoolboy says, "We won all our matches this term," meaning, not that he is personally a member of the team, but that what the team does is the achievement not of the team only but also of the school, so the Englishman says, "We won the battle of Trafalgar, we gave South Africa its constitution, and we have made no small contribution to art and science and letters." He would not imply thereby that he personally has made any observable contribution to these achievements; yet they are his because he is an Englishman. So the Christian says, "We spread over the Roman Empire; we defeated all the gods of paganism; we built up the great civilization of the Middle Ages; we have taken our Gospel to the ends of the earth; we have abolished infanticide and slavery; we shall yet abolish war"; for what the Church has done, all its members have done through participation in the common body.

Whatever may be the metaphysical nature of this quasi-personality of families and corporate bodies, this kind of language corresponds with spiritual fact. In the same way what Christ has done we that are His have done because we are His Body, His people, His family. In Him we have triumphed over sin and death, in Him we are righteous, in Him we stand before God unafraid.

The same spiritual fact may be stated in a more personal way. We are not individuals who really exist in isolation from those who are part of us. No man can be happy and carefree when those whom most he loves are in pain and sorrow. Thus, using, as we must, the language of symbolism, we may say that Christ stands before God as our great Representative, our Advocate; He cannot enter into Heaven (for it can be no heaven for Him) apart from those with whom He has so identified Himself in love that they are His brethren, part of His very self. The Second Adam cries:

No, no! I feel
The link of nature draw me; flesh of flesh,
Bone of my bone thou art, and from thy state
Mine never shall be parted, bliss or woe.

Our hope of salvation, both for ourselves and for all others, is not grounded upon any assurance either of our own merits or even of the stability of our own faith, but upon the assurance that He will not, and cannot, let us go, or, as it has been put, that He on the Cross with arms outstretched espoused to Himself the soul of every man, for better for worse, for richer for poorer, and death never shall them part. So to embrace humanity is not given to any man; yet it is integral to the Christian revelation in the Cross that God has so bound us to Himself with bonds that not sin nor shame nor death nor hell can break. He has taken our nature upon Him, the Incarnate Word has called us brethren, and thus is the Saviour of the world.

V

The appropriation of salvation

The dogma, then, that "Christ died for our sins according to the Scriptures" may be further defined. First, we are asserting not the death of a martyr, but the Crucifixion of the Incarnate Word. This stupendous conception implies that very God has entered into history – that He has borne our sins and our pains, that He has become one of us, that His blessedness is for ever linked with our salvation. Only when we have said that God *so* loved, do we know what it means that God is Love, for this is not an abstract proposition in philosophy, but the adoring apprehension of a saving act.

There still remains the question of our appropriation of this salvation. It is the abiding merit of the view associated with the great name of Abælard that it lays stress on the need of personal and inward change in us as the fruit of the sufferings of Christ. In taking our nature upon Him and espousing the cause of mankind, Christ has thrown open to all the gates of everlasting life. But the gates being open, we must enter. Christ's work *for* us must be completed by Christ's work *in* us. Moreover, it is no doubt psychologically and historically true that the contemplation of the love of God revealed on Calvary has softened the hearts of men and brought them to repentance and to faith. We are not personally saved until by faith we accept the love of God and are reconciled to Him.

"Sola fide"

But are we saved by faith and faith alone? This is supposed to be the doctrine of Protestants, while Romanists are deemed to hold that we are saved by faith and meritorious works. Into this long controversy we may not enter, nor may we aver that it is much ado about a trivial matter; but it would not be difficult to show that there has been great and unnecessary misunderstanding between the antagonists. If by faith we were to mean orthodoxy or the holding of any particular opinions, it could not with any propriety be said that we are saved by faith. But if it be meant that we are saved through faith in, and humble acceptance of, the immeasurable grace of the Incarnate Word, that is a truth which all Christians share. If Romanists have seemed to qualify the sole sufficiency of faith in Christ by reference to the merits of the saints, Protestants have been unwilling to recognize that there is any place for human merit in the Christian scheme. "Abound in good works," said the apostle, "knowing that your labour is not in vain in the Lord." "Cast not away your confidence which hath great recompense of reward." St. Paul could speak of that crown of victory which the Lord, the righteous judge, should give him "in that day"; and Christ promised to him who in His name should give a cup of cold water that he should not lose his reward, nor did he hesitate to speak of great "reward" in heaven. But there is, or should be, here no disharmony with the principle of faith alone. "God forbid," says the Council of Trent, "that a Christian man should trust or boast in himself and not in the Lord, of whose so great goodness towards men it is that He would have those things to be their merits which are His own gifts." We may also bear in mind the warning of Sir Thomas Browne: "Insolent zeals that do deny good works and rely only on faith take not away merit: for depending upon the efficacy of their faith they enforce the condition of God, and in a more sophistical way do seem to challenge Heaven."

The Cross as victory

That "Christ died for our sins according to the Scriptures" is a dogma of the faith, an integral element in the Christian "story." This form of words, however, might be interpreted to mean no more than the truism that Jesus Christ fell victim to the sins that beset mankind. That is an obvious fact of history, not an apprehension of adoring faith. In the Christian dogma we recognize the mighty act of God. We may describe the effects of this act upon our consciousness by speaking of the influence of Christ and of His Cross; but the act itself we can only describe in the form of narrative. The metaphor or analogy that stands nearest to the thought of the New Testament is that of Victory, for the Cross is not to be separated from the Resurrection. The Cross is the death-grapple of the eternal Son with the prince of darkness; by dying He destroyed the power of Death and Sin. Many other analogies are suggested in Scripture; most famous in Christian thought are that of a ransom paid whereby we are set free, and that of a sacrifice offered whereby our sin is expiated. We need not complain that to-day these two symbols are widely set aside, provided that with the rejection of the symbol we do not reject that which is symbolized.

The Cross as ransom

The great and permanent value of the theologies that rested upon the symbolism of a debt or ransom paid for us lies in the assertion that the Incarnate Word accomplished for us finally and for ever that which man for himself could never achieve, and that the Atonement, prior to any subjective appropriation of it on our part, is a mighty and saving act of God, a "finished work."

The Cross as sacrifice

The theology that rests upon the analogy of sacrifice has been repudiated, partly because it is supposed to imply that God punished His Son instead of punishing us, and partly because of a violent distaste for the symbolism of the "blood" of Christ. The conception of vicarious punishment is rejected on two grounds: first, that it is intrinsically immoral, and, second, that the old idea of vindictive punishment is giving way to that of remedial punishment which would be meaningless in relation to our Lord. The objection to the term "blood" is due almost entirely to misunderstanding. "Now the blood is the life." The vital part of the sacrifice here in mind was the application of the victim's blood to the altar or the lintel of the door or to the worshippers. The "blood" is a symbol for the life that has passed through death. When it is said, therefore, that we are "saved by the blood of Christ," this means neither more nor less than that we are saved by the living Crucified; it is, therefore, a compendious phrase for expressing that which must be the heart of any theology of the Atonement. Salvation by the blood of Christ – that is, by the living Christ who died for us – is an essential dogma of the faith, but it is not a necessary form of speech. Sacrifice means dedication through which union is effected between God and man; this is so exact an expression of the work of Christ that it was, and, wherever it is understood, is still, inevitable upon the lips of Christians.

That finished and not to be repeated victory achieved for us through the Crucifixion of the eternal Son is, in respect of its significance for the whole human race, well set forth in the theology that treats of the redemption of mankind through the assumption of human nature by the Word of God. But no theological theory is binding upon Christians, no explanation of the Cross is a Christian dogma. We may reject all the theologies of the Atonement, if we will, on the ground that they are inadequate to the mystery of the Crucifixion of Him who was God as well as man, but the mystery itself is at the heart of the Christian faith. Sin, we say, is such that only through the Redeemer's death could be inaugurated the New Covenant between God and man, could the Kingdom come, could sin be put away.

The sacraments

This reference to the New Covenant indicates the close connection between the Christian dogma and the Christian sacraments. I have written, recently, elsewhere at some length,[1] and may here refer to what I have written, about the sacraments. Sacraments are not dogmas. On the other hand, sacraments are "acts of God"; they are not *ex opere operantis*; they are the acts of Christ in and through His Church; they are Calvary, as it were, projected into later time and brought personally home to the recipient. They are part of the Gospel; they are the "story" brought down to our day and including us. This consideration leads inevitably to our final chapter on the Church.

[1] In *Christian Worship*, Clarendon Press, 1936.

CHAPTER XI

THE CHURCH CATHOLIC AND APOSTOLIC

I

IN view of the present divided state of Christianity it has been suggested that the creed should be amended so as to run: "I believe in the Holy Catholic Church, and I regret that it does not exist." The situation that gives rise to this witticism needs to be taken seriously, but not the amendment itself. Belief in the Holy Catholic Church is a dogma of the faith.

Easter and Pentecost

It is a dogma of the faith because dogma is correlative to the mighty acts of God. Elsewhere, in *The Defence of Christianity*,[1] I have sought to relate the idea of the Church to the teaching of our Lord. Here, however, we are chiefly concerned with the relations of Church and dogma. The Lord came into Galilee proclaiming the imminence of the Kingdom; in His words and works He showed that the Kingdom was actually operative amongst men, but His words and miracles did not in themselves constitute the whole of that supernatural intervention which He proclaimed. The New Covenant must be established through His death. But His death and Resurrection are not the end of the "story," for the Resurrection by itself, while it constitutes God's vindication of His Son, does not include the establishment of the heavenly Kingdom. As we cannot separate the Cross from the Resurrection, so we

[1] Eyre & Spottiswoode, 1936.

cannot separate the Resurrection from the sending of the Holy Ghost. Easter is followed by Pentecost.

The close connection between Easter and Pentecost is shown by the statement in the Fourth Gospel that the Risen Lord breathed upon His disciples, and said unto them: "Receive ye the Holy Ghost." I have dealt elsewhere (in the *Queen's Quarterly*, Vol. XXXVII.) with the technical obscurities of the Pentecost narrative or narratives in Acts; for our present purpose these are of little importance. The vital matter is that after the Resurrection the coming of the Kingdom is not a sudden momentary act, but a process that begins with the descent of the Holy Ghost and ends with the final consummation. The term "Church," therefore, may be taken to cover those elements in the creed which have not hitherto been discussed.

The Church visible and invisible

The life and death of our Lord have touched the conscience of mankind, so that His Name is honoured and reverenced even where the Christian faith is not professed. But the Church that is called by His Name does not share in this regard. There are even Christians who sharply distinguish between Christ and His Church, and are disposed to contrast organized Christianity as a whole with the spirit and purpose of its Lord. This takes the form of a clear distinction between the Church visible and the Church invisible; the Church visible, it is maintained, consists of all baptized persons or all Churchgoers, and thus includes many who show no signs of having received the Spirit; the Church invisible, on the other hand, consists of the saints or those who are truly Christian in mind and temper, and is thus often taken to include not only many who sit loose to organized Christianity, but some who would even repudiate the Christian name. Thus the Church of faith is sharply distinguished from the Church as organized on earth.

The ground for this distinction lies in the sad and often tragic history of the Church, her misunderstandings of her Lord, her disloyalty, her dreadful worldliness. Viewed from without, the Church appears an all too human institution. But the proper distinction between the Church visible and the Church invisible is not at all as is here supposed. The dogma, " I believe in the Holy Catholic Church," does not mean, " I believe in the ideal, as distinct from the actual, Church " ; it means, rather, " I believe in the one actual Church in heaven and on earth as the work of God and the Body of Christ."

It must be freely admitted that some may belong to the body of the Church who do not belong to her soul, and that some are outside the body who assuredly belong to the soul, but this has nothing to do with the visibility and invisibility of the Church. The hiddenness, the *incognito*, in the life of Christ has its reflection in the hiddenness, the *incognito*, in the life of His disciples. As the incarnate life of God was hidden in man, so the regenerate life of man is hidden in God. Though Christians may let their light shine before men, and many of the triumphs of the Cross are for all to see, yet the life of the Church is a hidden life.

It is often said that those who make no profession of faith are just as good as, or even better than, many professing Christians. Doubtless some Christians are such only in name, but can we say that many who make no profession of faith are better than the ordinary Christian ? If it is a question of weighing merit, we have no scales for the purpose and little enough to weigh. No Christian should wish to claim that his life is more meritorious than that of his pagan friend, but there is an eternal difference between the life that is "in Christ" and the life that is not "in Christ." If many a pagan performs more "good works," than many a penitent and feeble Christian, which is more acceptable in the eyes of God – the morality of the one, or the broken and contrite heart of the other? "Nobody knows the troubles I've had," says the negro song. Nobody knows the temptations, struggles, defeats, victories, prayers, tears, graces, consolations of any Christian heart. The life of the soul is a hidden life. The Lord knows them that are His. Many a saint travels through all his pilgrimage *incognito*. The man who in spite of all his sins and imperfections acknowledges and accepts the infinite grace and condescension of God in Jesus Christ his Saviour is in principle right with God or justified and accepted, though the road to sanctification be still long and hard. The man who acknowledges no Saviour and recognizes no need of a Saviour is still, for all his good works, in his pride and in his sins. The Church consists not of the good, but of the redeemed. This truth is symbolized and ratified in the sacrament of baptism, which is the door into the Church.

The Church visible on earth is a company of weak and sinful and ignorant men and women, divided amongst themselves, showing many evidences of the spirit of the world, and organized in institutions like those of society at large. The Church invisible on earth is that same company of people viewed as those who belong to the covenant of grace, have received the Holy Spirit, and are members of that Body whose Head is Christ. This is the dogma of the Church. The firstfruits of the mighty act of God in Jesus Christ is the new Israel, the people of God, the holy Church.

The relation of the Church to the Word or Gospel is twofold: not only is the Church the community that

The Church and the Word

declares the Word; it is also itself constituted by, and is even an extension of, the very mighty act of God which it declares. This relation to the Gospel enables us to define what the term "Church" must mean. The fundamental principle is that the Gospel is not so much that which the Church proclaims as the Church is that which proclaims the Gospel. In other words, we must relate our conception of the Church to the New Testament, of which it is the continuation. An essential mark, therefore, of the Church is continuity. The Church is part of the mighty act of God in the redemption of mankind by the imparting of the supernatural Spirit through the work of the Incarnate Word. Resurrection – Holy Spirit – Church are inseparable ideas. The Church is constituted by the believing of the Word, the receiving of the Spirit, the preaching of the Word, and the administration of the sacraments.

Protestants, who have been wont to find in the New Testament not only the unchanging Gospel of the Church and the standard and rule of faith, but also the ideal formal organization of the Church and sole illustration of Christianity in its purity, have tended to regard the whole subsequent history of the Church, which conquered the Roman Empire, civilised Europe, gave us St. Bernard and St. Francis, Dante and St. Thomas, as an ever further declension from the mind of Christ and the influence of the Spirit. Thus they virtually suppose that true Christianity appeared with the apostles and then reappeared, as one recovered from an almost mortal sickness, in the sixteenth century. They are consequently apt to consider the Mediæval Church as "the Roman Catholic Church" in which they have no lot and no desirable inheritance, and many go so far as largely to repudiate the Reformers on the ground that they are too "Catholic" or mediæval. It is the just recognition of the Church's continuity which gives religious significance to the doctrine of the Apostolical Succession.

The notes of the Church

The term "catholic" or "universal" is strictly correlative to the Word, the Gospel, the teaching or dogma. They are catholics who hold the catholic faith and live the catholic life. The catholicity of the Church, the unity of the Church, and the holiness of the Church are indissolubly connected with the Word of God which is the Christian "story." The Church arises from "the story" because it is the continuation of the story, the work of the Holy Spirit; it knows itself as the Church because it believes the Gospel and experiences the supernatural life. The unity of the Church is not something to be created or achieved, but something to be expressed; it is constituted by the common faith and the common supernatural life. So, too, the holiness of the Church is due not to the meritoriousness of its members, but to the divine life of the Risen Lord present in the Spirit. So, also, the apostolicity of the Church is derived from the Word; for the Church possesses this attribute by abiding in the doctrine and life of the Apostles, in their doctrine as believing the Word, in their life as quickened by the Holy Spirit that descended at Pentecost and constitutes the Church, the work and "mighty act" of God.

Thus holiness, catholicity, unity, and apostolicity are necessary marks of the Church, and this, not only in idea, but metaphysically. By this I mean that the Church not only declares the Word of God from the past, but is in the present a metaphysical entity whose true life is Christ; the Church not only expounds a tradition, but lives a supernatural life which is the continuation of that redemptive act of God which itself constitutes the tradition.

This is the mystery of the Church – that it is both visible and invisible ; that it is both of earth and heaven ; that it both is not, and yet is, the Bride of Christ, His sacred Body. There is this parallel between the life of the incarnate Lord and the life of the incarnate Church, that for both there is a purely historical side, and in both the divinity is hidden ; but there is this great difference, that whereas the Lord is very God and very man, yet without sin, the Church is very Spirit and yet all too human with many stains of human sin. The Church consists of those who are saved because they are in Christ, but are still being saved because the work of their sanctification is far from complete.

The sphere of the Holy Spirit

The goal of the Church as the sphere of the Holy Spirit is the perfect sanctification of souls, but the Church itself is not a fellowship of an *élite*. Calvin violently repudiated the doctrine of the Cathari, who said that only the pure could be members of the Church. One of the characters in Ida Friederike Coudenhove's book, *The Burden of Belief*, speaks thus : " Do you realize that this brings us to the vital problem of the *masses* in the Church ? Granted everything that you have said (and which of us has not felt the same thing ?), yet the fact that it is so is not only something to depress us and fill us with shame ; it is something to fortify our faith. Yes, I mean it, it is a spectacle which, when I contemplate it, sometimes makes me want to fall down on my knees in reverent devotion : for here I see how utterly God threw everything into the hazard when He delivered Himself up to reality, and the truly terrifying, humble, heroic obedience of the Church which dares to take upon herself the burden of humanity just as it is, to deliver herself up to it, to expose herself to a martyrdom of degradation, which one who basks in the kingdom of the ' pure idea ' would never dream of. . . . That I call taking the mystery of the Incarnation seriously. It is its final consequence. With the stern and solemn passion which she reserves for combating heresy, the Church has always unceasingly resisted the great temptation which has pursued her through the centuries, from Montanus and Tertullian to Port Royal, and which still survives among many of us to-day, although we have no name for it – and in truth it is not the basest natures that have succumbed and do succumb to it – the great temptation to become in any sense the Church of an *élite* – of the ' philosophers,' of the ' saints,' of the ' pure,' of the ' Charismatics.' Always has she preferred to endure the reproaches of degeneration and apostasy, to be accused of being false to her mission, of doing violence to her Founder (think of the Grand Inquisitor !), of entering into cowardly and cunning compromise with the world and sin and stupidity and error – and, behold, she answers with the legion of her saints. . . . And your question, too, comes in here : Do you see what it means if the Church really exists *for all* ? It means that she allows and encourages everyone to set out on the road to her ideal of perfection, even though he takes along with him the queerest baggage : stupidity (how much has that alone been responsible for in the history of piety !) and bad taste and inner vulgarity, narrowness and fanaticism, and in the case of every single individual, without exception, the whole encumbrance of a nature as yet unpurified and uncontrolled, and prone at all times to error, sudden freakishness, and acts of betrayal."

There is danger lest those who hold this view should make the principle of the Incarnation an excuse for the Church's sin and shame. The Church is not the incarnation of the Spirit in the sense in which Christ is the incarnation of the Word. Christ is perfect God and perfect man; the Church is perfect Spirit and very imperfect men. In mediæval as well as modern times, as is indicated by the monastic movement and the history of the Free Churches, men have felt the compelling force of the injunction, "Come ye out from among them, and be ye separate." If this has often meant schism and breach of Church fellowship, it may be thought that the fault lies chiefly with the corrupted body. Schism is always a sin, but it is not always the sin of the ejected.

II

If, then, "the Holy Catholic Church" is to be understood of the empirical or actual Church, not of the idea of the Church, there are two principles by which the limits of the Church may be defined – the principle of the hierarchy and the principle of the Word.

The principle of the hierarchy

The former asserts that where the hierarchy is, there is the Church. There are serious defects to this principle. First, it is not derived from Scripture, which is the standard and rule of faith. Second, it is impossible to show, for instance, that the Church of England is, and the Church of Scotland or the Methodist Church is not, a part of the Holy Catholic Church except by the method of *petitio principii* or bare assertion. Third, if it be maintained that bishops in the Succession are necessary to guarantee the purity of the Word, the validity of the Sacraments and the unity of the Church, the answer lies to hand that the guarantee has proved itself unsatisfactory, and that on any showing the essence of the Church must lie in that which is guaranteed, not in the guarantors.

In accordance with their fundamental principle Protestants reply that the episcopate at its best is the servant and minister of the Word, not part of it. It is the Word that imparts authority to bishops, it is not they who guarantee the Word; it is the sacraments of the Word that make valid their ministry, not their ministry that makes valid the sacraments. While the Christian "story" cannot be told without reference to the mighty acts of the Holy Spirit in the Church, much of the Church's story (and that not the least triumphant part) can and must be told without reference to bishops. On the other hand, it should be frankly recognised by Protestants that the intransigent insistence upon "the historic episcopate" rests at the present time upon religious insights which in themselves are fundamental in Christianity, and which in the existing state of Protestantism are in grave danger of being overlooked. The unity and continuity of the Church and the recognition of the supernatural in the Church's life are not side-issues. Our protest is not against that which episcopacy represents, but only against that view which would make Word and Sacrament contingent upon the office, not the office on the Word.

The principle of the Word

The only alternative to definition by the hierarchy is definition by the Word. The Holy Catholic Church is defined by the Gospel which it proclaims, and which creates it ever anew. The Church is that fellowship wherein the Christian "story" is proclaimed and believed, where, in the sacraments of the Word, the promise of Christ is confirmed and sealed to the individual believer in the fellowship of believers, and where that Holy Spirit dwells that was given in the mighty act of God which we celebrate at Easter and at Pentecost.

But how shall we so work out this principle as to avoid the Pharisaism of a Church of the *élite*? It can be no part of my task, since it is wholly beyond my competence, to decide at what point a community ceases by defection to be part of the Body of Christ, or at what point a man so falls away from his baptism that he ceases to be a member of the Church. The principle, however hard it be of particular application, stands clear – that the Church consists of believers and their children, and is constituted by that Word of God which is declared in Scripture, defined in the creeds, and confirmed in the sacraments. As a practical, but not as a final or divinely guaranteed, rule the Church consists of the baptized. But how shall we determine whether or not a communion faithfully preaches the Word and administers the sacraments? How gladly would we all embrace episcopacy, if it carried with it a guarantee of so great a benefit! The only answer must be that the Lord judges hearts and not we, but that any community which professes its faith in the Word of God declared in Scripture and defined in the creeds and confessions of the Church must be deemed a part of the Church Catholic, unless its profession be manifestly insincere or its life manifestly deny its faith.

The Congregational idea

It will, I am sure, be said that, in abandoning the idea of the Church as consisting of the *élite*, I have by implication repudiated the conception of a Congregational Church, and have made havoc of its claim to be self-governing. Let me, therefore, make quite clear what I conceive to be the truth in the witness of that section of Christendom through which I belong to the Great Church.

It was, I believe, at the call of God and under the guidance of His Spirit that in earlier days men retired from "the world" into the monastic life. In evil days the monasteries may have been the glowing centres of the Church's life, but they were not coextensive with the Church. Similarly a Congregational Church (or a Methodist denomination) is a close fellowship or religious order of those who are separated by God for the disciplined life of a fellowship at a higher level than the whole Church has attained. These fellowships are not coextensive with the whole Church, but they are a part of it that is of inestimable spiritual importance. That, unlike the monasteries, the Protestant denominations should be out of fellowship and communion with some part of the Church is tragic. If little or no blame attaches for this to those who went out or who were forced out for conscience' sake, great blame would attach to those who should remain out in a satisfied isolation. There is schism in the Body; all sections are to blame for this, and repentance is required of all. A Congregational Church (or Methodist denomination) is now at this moment, like the Church of England, a fellowship within the Great Church. The Church is one, but her unity, which is created by the Word, lacks appropriate expression in outward form and common life.

Moreover, the Congregational principle of the autonomy of the local fellowship, when correctly stated, is fully justified. By definition such a fellowship consists of those who have received the Holy Ghost, have been instructed in the faith, have entered into covenant with one another and with their Lord to walk in His ways and to obey His commandments, living no more unto themselves but unto Him, the only Head of the Church. Such a community, wholly subject to the Word and filled with the living Spirit, is in virtue of the Spirit's presence and the promise of the Lord to be in the midst of the two or three who are gathered in His Name, competent to order all its internal affairs, subject only to the needs and admonitions of the whole Church catholic. It is to be remembered that the secular democratic principle of one man one vote with the remission of all issues to the whole membership is not Congregationalism. There can only be a properly constituted Congregational Church where there are ministers, elders, and deacons set apart in virtue of their spiritual gifts and accepted as the ministers of Christ to the Church. The Congregational principle is the extension to the local congregation of that liberty which Luther claimed for the individual Christian. It is a principle of responsibility, not of isolation. How far Congregational Churches, as they exist at present, fulfil the conditions requisite for the operation of their principle, is a matter beyond my competence.

III

The paradox of the Church

In my booklet, *The Church Catholic*, I have written further about the political and ecclesiastical aspects of the Church, and of her task and calling. Here I return to the Church as belonging to the sphere of Christian faith and dogma. We are confronted with a staggering paradox – that the Church is the mighty work of God, the firstfruits of the coming of the Kingdom, and that it is at the same time that very imperfect corporation of which we read in European history; or, to put the matter in another way, the Christian Church, as we know it, is divided, worldly, stupid, corrupt, apathetic, stuffy, and at the same time it is the Bride of Christ, His sacred Body. The Church is not the Body of Christ because her members are good or wise or even nice, but because she believes in Christ, and He is her true and hidden life. From without we may see in the Church of the subapostolic age a sad falling off from the first radiance of the apostolic days, a tragic failure to understand the apostle Paul, the rapid growth of formalism and superstition. And this was the Church of the martyrs that without prestige or any worldly influence spread across the Empire, proved itself stronger than all paganisms and mightier than Rome! What crimes and sins, ignorance and superstition, blacken the story of the Church in the Dark and Middle Ages! Yet this is the Church not merely of unnumbered saints and heroes, but the Church that brought all human thought into obedience to Christ, put the holy Mother of God in the place of the ancient lascivious goddess of fertility, taught mercy, pity, and peace in the Name of the Crucified to the savage tribes of Europe, sought to order society upon the sure foundation of the laws of God, and bade the hearts of men to look in faith and hope beyond the passing fashions of this transitory world! We are critical of the Church Roman, Protestant, Oriental in the generations just gone by, as we are apt to be disdainful of the Church divided, and seemingly impotent, that struggles in the morass to-day; yet the past hundred years has seen some of the greatest triumphs of the Cross since the days of Pentecost! The Church is a wonderful and sacred mystery, an all too human institution which hides a divine and supernatural life against which the gates of hell shall not prevail.

The least of Christians may be aware of this supernatural and hidden life within himself. He would never dream of regarding himself as a better man than his pagan neighbour, but he is used and blessed as the pagan cannot be. There is an eternal difference between the world on the one side and, on the other, those who look to Christ and acknowledge Him as Lord – however dim their eyes and weak their wills. The mystery of this hidden life is intimately associated with the sacraments of baptism and of the Holy Supper (concerning which I may refer to my paper in *Christian Worship*), not that these rites in themselves are anything, but that in the context of the Church and of faith they are the symbols and vehicles of the supernatural life.

The Church triumphant

The Church is a great company of which a small part lingers on this side of the River. There are dogmas of which I have said nothing. In particular I have been silent about that country and that Vision which is the Christian's hope. Silence does not mean that these things may be deemed of secondary importance. It is better to meditate on the Saint's Everlasting Rest than to labour with problems of theology; but of these matters it is not possible to write in the style that has seemed appropriate to these discussions. Nor would it become me to attempt to write of ascetical theology or that life of God in the soul of man which presupposes the faith in the Son of God. "*Lex orandi*," says Walter Pater, "*lex credendi* – our creeds are but the brief abstract of our prayers and song." It is in our prayers that our dogmas come to life. But I have written enough to make my one point clear.

I started from the questions, "What precisely is the Christian Faith?" and, "How shall we distinguish its changing form from its enduring substance?" I have replied that in essence the Christian faith is not a theory or philosophy but a recapitulation of "the mighty acts of God"; it is "the old, old story"; it may be told in ten thousand different ways, but it is ever one recognizable story of the divine Charity, the heavenly Condescension, the Redemption of mankind through God made man. This story may be summarized in the saying that "God so loved the world, that He gave His only begotten Son, that whosoever believeth in Him should not perish, but have everlasting life." When the implications of this summary are worked out, the resultant "story" has many moments, corresponding to the acts of God. It begins with the Creation; there follow the call of Abraham, the sending of the Prophets, the Incarnation of the Son, His Cross, His Resurrection, the sending of the Holy Ghost, the calling and commission of the Christian Church; it ends with the Consummation, when all that came into being through the Son returns to the Father through the Son, and the redeemed creation in the unveiled Presence joins in the eternal worship to Father, Son, and Holy Ghost.

As all Christian doctrine is summed up in the dogma of the Trinity, so is all involved in the mystery of God made man. *Credo ut intelligam* – I believe that I may understand. "Lord, I believe; help Thou mine unbelief!"

APPENDIX

THE APOSTLES' CREED

I BELIEVE in God the Father Almighty, Maker of heaven and earth:

And in Jesus Christ his only Son our Lord, Who was conceived by the Holy Ghost, Born of the Virgin Mary, Suffered under Pontius Pilate, Was crucified, dead and buried, He descended into hell; The third day he rose again from the dead, He ascended into heaven, And sitteth on the right hand of God the Father Almighty; from thence he shall come to judge the quick and the dead.

I BELIEVE in the Holy Ghost; The holy Catholick Church; the Communion of Saints; The Forgiveness of sins; The Resurrection of the body, And the life everlasting.

THE NICENE CREED

I BELIEVE in one God the Father Almighty, Maker of heaven and earth, And of all things visible and invisible:

And in one Lord Jesus Christ, the only-begotten Son of God, Begotten of his Father before all worlds, God of God, Light of Light, Very God of very God, Begotten, not made, Being of one substance with the Father, By whom all things were made: Who for us men, and for our salvation came down from heaven, And was incarnate by the Holy Ghost of the Virgin Mary, And was made man, And was crucified also for us under Pontius Pilate. He suffered and was buried, And the third day he rose again according to the Scriptures, And ascended into heaven,

And sitteth on the right hand of the Father. And he shall come again with glory to judge both the quick and the dead : Whose kingdom shall have no end.

AND I BELIEVE in the Holy Ghost, The Lord and Giver of life, Who proceedeth from the Father and the Son, Who with the Father and the Son together is worshipped and glorified, Who spake by the Prophets. And I believe one Catholick and Apostolick Church. I acknowledge one Baptism for the remission of sins. And I look for the Resurrection of the dead, And the life of the world to come.

INDEX

INDEX

INDEX